6th Web as Corpus Workshop 2010

(WAC-6)

Held at NAACL HLT 2010

Los Angeles, California, USA
5 June 2010

ISBN: 978-1-61738-684-8

Printed from e-media with permission by:

Curran Associates, Inc.
57 Morehouse Lane
Red Hook, NY 12571

Some format issues inherent in the e-media version may also appear in this print version.

Printed by Curran Associates, Inc. (2010)

Association for Computational Linguistics
209 N. Eighth Street
Stroudsburg, Pennsylvania 18360

Phone: 1-570-476-8006
Fax: 1-570-476-0860

acl@aclweb.org

Additional copies of this publication are available from:

Curran Associates, Inc.
57 Morehouse Lane
Red Hook, NY 12571 USA
Phone: 845-758-0400
Fax: 845-758-2634
Email: curran@proceedings.com
Web: www.proceedings.com

Introduction

More and more people are using Web data for linguistic and NLP research. The workshop, the sixth in an annual series, provides a venue for exploring how we can use it effectively and what we will find if we do, with particular attention to

- Web corpus collection projects, or modules for one part of the process (crawling, filtering, de-duplication, language-id, tokenising, indexing, ...)
- characteristics of Web data from a linguistics/NLP perspective including registers, domains, frequency distributions, comparisons between datasets
- using crawled Web data for NLP purposes (with emphasis on the data rather than the use)

Previous WAC workshops have been in Europe and Africa. The west coast of the US is the global centre for web development, hosting Google, Microsoft, Yahoo and a thousand others, so we are glad to be here!

Organizers:

Adam Kilgarriff, Lexical Computing Ltd. (Workshop Chair)
Dekang Lin, Google Inc.
Serge Sharoff, University of Leeds (SIGWAC Chair)

Program Committee:

Adam Kilgarriff, Lexical Computing Ltd. (UK)
Dekang Lin, Google Inc. (USA)
Serge Sharoff, University of Leeds (UK)
Silvia Bernardini, University of Bologna (Italy)
Stefan Evert, University of Osnabrück (Germany)
Cédrick Fairon, UCLouvain (Belgium)
William H. Fletcher, U.S. Naval Academy (USA)
Gregory Grefenstette, Exalead, (France)
Igor Leturia, Elhuyar Fundazioa (Spain)
Jan Pomikálek, Masaryk University (Czech Republic)
Preslav Nakov, National University of Singapore
Kevin Scannell, Saint Louis University (USA)
Gilles-Maurice de Schryver, Ghent University (Belgium)

Invited Speaker:

Patrick Pantel, ISI, University of Southern California

Proceedings:

Jan Pomikálek

Table of Contents

Workshop Program

Saturday, June 5, 2010

	Session 1:
8:30	Start, introduction
8:40	*NoWaC: a large web-based corpus for Norwegian* Emiliano Raul Guevara
9:05	*Building a Korean Web Corpus for Analyzing Learner Language* Markus Dickinson, Ross Israel and Sun-Hee Lee
9:30	Invited talk by Patrick Pantel
10:30	Coffee break
	Session 2:
11:00	*Sketching Techniques for Large Scale NLP* Amit Goyal, Jagadeesh Jagaralamudi, Hal Daumé III and Suresh Venkatasubramanian
11:25	*Building Webcorpora of Academic Prose with BootCaT* George Dillon
11:50	*Google Web 1T 5-Grams Made Easy (but not for the computer)* Stefan Evert
12:15	Closing session

NoWaC: a large web-based corpus for Norwegian

Emiliano Guevara
Tekstlab,
Institute for Linguistics and Nordic Studies,
University of Oslo
e.r.guevara@iln.uio.no

Abstract

In this paper we introduce the first version of *noWaC*, a large web-based corpus of Bokmål Norwegian currently containing about 700 million tokens. The corpus has been built by crawling, downloading and processing web documents in the *.no* top-level internet domain. The procedure used to collect the *noWaC* corpus is largely based on the techniques described by Ferraresi et al. (2008). In brief, first a set of "seed" URLs containing documents in the target language is collected by sending queries to commercial search engines (Google and Yahoo). The obtained seeds (overall 6900 URLs) are then used to start a crawling job using the Heritrix web-crawler limited to the *.no* domain. The downloaded documents are then processed in various ways in order to build a linguistic corpus (e.g. filtering by document size, language identification, duplicate and near duplicate detection, etc.).

1 Introduction and motivations

The development, training and testing of NLP tools requires suitable electronic sources of linguistic data (corpora, lexica, treebanks, ontological databases, etc.), which demand a great deal of work in order to be built and are, very often copyright protected. Furthermore, the ever growing importance of heavily data-intensive NLP techniques for strategic tasks such as machine translation and information retrieval, has created the additional requirement that these electronic resources be very large and general in scope.

Since most of the current work in NLP is carried out with data from the economically most impacting languages (and especially with English data), an amazing wealth of tools and resources is available for them. However, researchers interested in "smaller" languages (whether by the number of speakers or by their market relevance in the NLP industry) must struggle to transfer and adapt the available technologies because the suitable sources of data are lacking. Using the web as corpus is a promising option for the latter case, since it can provide with reasonably large and reliable amounts of data in a relatively short time and with a very low production cost.

In this paper we present the first version of *noWaC*, a large web-based corpus of Bokmål Norwegian, a language with a limited web presence, built by crawling the *.no* internet top level domain. The computational procedure used to collect the *noWaC* corpus is by and large based on the techniques described by Ferraresi et al. (2008). Our initiative was originally aimed at collecting a 1.5–2 billion word general-purpose corpus comparable to the corpora made available by the WaCky initiative (`http://wacky.sslmit.unibo.it`). However, carrying out this project on a language with a relatively small online presence such as Bokmål has lead to results which differ from previously reported similar projects. In its current, first version, *noWaC* contains about 700 million tokens.

Proceedings of the NAACL HLT 2010 Sixth Web as Corpus Workshop, pages 1–7,
Los Angeles, California, June 2010.

1.1 Norwegian: linguistic situation and available corpora

Norway is a country with a population of ca. 4.8 million inhabitants that has two official national written standards: *Bokmål* and *Nynorsk* (respectively, 'book language' and 'new Norwegian'). Of the two standards, Bokmål is the most widely used, being actively written by about 85% of the country's population (cf. `http://www.sprakrad.no/` for detailed up to date statistics). The two written standards are extremely similar, especially from the point of view of their orthography. In addition, Norway recognizes a number of regional minority languages (the largest of which, North Sami, has ca. 15,000 speakers).

While the written language is generally standardized, the spoken language in Norway is not, and using one's dialect in any occasion is tolerated and even encouraged. This tolerance is rapidly extending to informal writing, especially in modern means of communication and media such as internet forums, social networks, etc.

There is a fairly large number of corpora of the Norwegian language, both spoken and written (in both standards). However, most of them are of a limited size (under 50 million words, cf. `http://www.hf.uio.no/tekstlab/` for an overview). To our knowledge, the largest existing written corpus of Norwegian is the *Norsk Aviskorpus* (Hofland 2000, cf. `http://avis.uib.no/`), an expanding newspaper-based corpus currently containing 700 million words. However, the *Norsk Aviskorpus* is only available though a dedicated web interface for non commercial use, and advanced research tasks cannot be freely carried out on its contents.

Even though we have only worked on building a web corpus for Bokmål Norwegian, we intend to apply the same procedures to create web-corpora also for Nynorsk and North Sami, thus covering the whole spectrum of written languages in Norway.

1.2 Obtaining legal clearance

The legal status of openly accessible web-documents is not clear. In practice, when one visits a web page with a browsing program, an electronic exact copy of the remote document is created locally; this logically implies that any online document must be, at least to a certain extent, copyright-free if it is to be visited/viewed at all. This is a major difference with respect to other types of documents (e.g. printed materials, films, music records) which cannot be copied at all.

However, when building a web corpus, we do not only wish to visit (i.e. download) web documents, but we would like to process them in various ways, index them and, finally, make them available to other researchers and users in general. All of this would ideally require clearance from the copyright holders of each single document in the corpus, something which is simply impossible to realize for corpora that contain millions of different documents.[1]

In short, web corpora are, from the legal point of view, still a very dark spot in the field of computational linguistics. In most countries, there is simply no legal background to refer to, and the internet is a sort of no-man's land.

Norway is a special case: while the law explicitly protects online content as intellectual property, there is rather new piece of legislation in *Forskrift til åndsverkloven av 21.12 2001 nr. 1563, § 1-4* that allows universities and other research institutions to ask for permission from the Ministry of Culture and Church in order to use copyright protected documents for research purposes that do not cause conflict with the right holders' own use or their economic interests (cf. `http://www.lovdata.no/cgi-wift/ldles?ltdoc=/for/ff-20011221-1563.html`). We have been officially granted this permission for this project, and we can proudly say that *noWaC* is a totally legal and recognized initiative. The results of this work will be legally made available free of charge for research (i.e. non commercial) purposes. *NoWaC* will be distributed in association with the *WaCky* initiative and also directly from the University of Oslo.

[1] Search engines are in a clear contradiction to the copyright policies in most countries: they crawl, download and index billions of documents with no clearance whatsoever, and also redistribute whole copies of the cached documents.

2 Building a corpus of Bokmål by web-crawling

2.1 Methods and tools

In this project we decided to follow the methods used to build the *WaCky* corpora, and to use the related tools as much as possible (e.g. the *BootCaT tools*). In particular, we tried to reproduce the procedures described by Ferraresi et al. (2008) and Baroni et al. (2009). The methodology has already produced web-corpora ranging from 1.7 to 2.6 billion tokens (German, Italian, British English). However, most of the steps needed some adaptation, fine-tuning and some extra programming. In particular, given the relatively complex linguistic situation in Norway, a step dedicated to document language identification was added.

In short, the building and processing chain used for *noWaC* comprises the following steps:

1. Extraction of list of mid-frequency Bokmål words from Wikipedia and building query strings
2. Retrieval of seed URLs from search engines by sending automated queries, limited to the *.no* top-level domain
3. Crawling the web using the seed URLS, limited to the *.no* top-level domain
4. Removing HTML boilerplate and filtering documents by size
5. Removing duplicate and near-duplicate documents
6. Language identification and filtering
7. Tokenisation
8. POS-tagging

At the time of writing, the first version of *noWaC* is being POS-tagged and will be made available in the course of the next weeks.

2.2 Retrieving seed URLs from search engines

We started by obtaining the Wikipedia text dumps for Bokmål Norwegian and related languages (Nynorsk, Danish, Swedish and Icelandic) and selecting the 2000 most frequent words that are unique to Bokmål. We then sent queries of 2 randomly selected Bokmål words though search engine APIs (Google and Yahoo!). A maximum of ten seed URLs were saved for each query, and the retrieved URLs were collapsed in a single list of root URLs, deduplicated and filtered, only keeping those in the *.no* top level domain.

After one week of automated queries (limited to 1000 queries per day per search engine by the respective APIs) we had about 6900 filtered seed URLs.

2.3 Crawling

We used the *Heritrix* open-source, web-scale crawler (`http://crawler.archive.org/`) seeded with the 6900 URLs we obtained to traverse the internet *.no* domain and to download only HTML documents (all other document types were discarded from the archive). We instructed the crawler to use a multi-threaded breadth-first strategy, and to follow a very strict politeness policy, respecting all `robots.txt` exclusion directives while downloading pages at a moderate rate (90 second pause before retrying any URL) in order not to disrupt normal website activity.

The final crawling job was stopped after 15 days. In this period of time, a total size of 1 terabyte was crawled, with approximately 90 million URLs being processed by the crawler. Circa 17 million HTML documents were downloaded, adding up to an overall archive size of 550 gigabytes. Only about 13.5 million documents were successfully retrieved pages (the rest consisting of various "page not found" replies and other server-side error messages).

The documents in the archive were filtered by size, keeping only those documents that were between 5Kb and 200Kb in size (following Ferraresi et al. 2008 and Baroni et al. 2009). This resulted in a reduced archive of 11.4 million documents for post-processing.

2.4 Post-processing: removing HTML boilerplate and de-duplication

At this point of the process, the archive contained raw HTML documents, still very far from being a linguistic corpus. We used the BootCaT toolkit (Baroni and Bernardini 2004, cf. `http://sslmit.unibo.it/~baroni/bootcat.html`) to perform the major operations to clean our archive.

First, every document was processed with the HTML boilerplate removal tool in order to select only the linguistically interesting portions of text while removing all HTML, Javascript and CSS code and non-linguistic material (made mainly of HTML tags, visual formatting, tables, navigation links, etc.)

Then, the archive was processed with the duplicate and near-duplicate detecting script in the the BootCaT toolkit, based on a 5-gram model. This is a very drastic strategy leading to a huge reduction in the number of kept documents: any two documents sharing more than 1/25 5-grams were considered duplicates, and both documents were discarded. The overall number of documents in the archive went down from 11.40 to 1.17 million after duplicate removal.[2]

2.5 Language identification and filtering

The complex linguistic situation in Norway makes us expect that the Norwegian internet be at least a bilingual domain (Bokmål and Nynorsk). In addition, we also expect a number of other languages to be present to a lesser degree.

We used Damir Cavar's tri-gram algorithm for language identification (cf. `http://ling.unizd.hr/~dcavar/LID/`), training 16 language models on Wikipedia text from languages that are closely related to, or that have contact with Bokmål (Bokmål, Danish, Dutch, English, Faeroese, Finnish, French, German, Icelandic, Italian, Northern Sami, Nynorsk, Polish, Russian, Spanish and Swedish). The best models were trained on 1Mb of random Wikipedia lines and evaluated against a database of one hundred 5 Kb article excerpts for each language. The models performed very well, often approaching 100% accuracy; however, the extremely similar orthography of Bokmål and Nynorsk make them the most difficult pair of languages to spot for the system, one being often misclassified as the other. In any case, our results were relatively good: *Bokmål* Precision = 1.00, Recall = 0.89, F-measure = 0.94, *Nynorsk* Precision = 0.90, Recall = 1.00, F-measure = 0.95.

The language identifying filter was applied on a document basis, recognizing about 3 out of 4 documents as Bokmål:

- 72.25% Bokmål
- 16.00% Nynorsk
- 05.80% English
- 02.43% Danish
- 01.95% Swedish

This filter produced another sensible drop in the overall number of kept documents: from 1.17 to 0.85 million.

2.6 POS-tagging and lemmatization

At the time of writing *noWaC* is in the process of being POS-tagged. This is not at all an easy task, since the best and most widely used tagger for Norwegian (the Oslo-Bergen tagger, cf. Hagen et al. 2000) is available as a binary distribution which, besides not being open to modifications, is fairly slow and does not handle large text files. A number of statistical taggers have been trained, but we are still undecided about which system to use because the available training materials for Bokmål are rather limited (about 120,000 words). The tagging accuracy we have obtained so far is still not comparable to the state-of-the-art (94.32% with TnT, 94.40% with SVMT). In addition, we are also working on creating a large list of tagged lemmas to be used with *noWaC*. We estimate that a final POS-tagged and lemmatized version of the corpus will be available in the next few weeks (in any case, before the WAC6 workshop).

3 Comparing results

While it is still too early for us to carry out a fully fledged qualitative evaluation of *noWaC*, we are able to compare our results with previous published work, especially with the WaCky corpora we tried to emulate.

3.1 NoWaC and the WaCky corpora

As we stated above, we tried to follow the WaCky methodology as closely as possible, in the hopes that we could obtain a very large corpus (we aimed at collecting above 1 billion tokens). However, even though our crawling job produced a much bigger initial archive than those reported for German, Italian and British English in Baroni et al. (2009), and

[2]As pointed out by an anonymous reviewer, this drastic reduction in number of documents may be due to faults in the boilerplate removal phase, leading to 5-grams of HTML or similar code counting as real text. We are aware of this issue, and the future versions of *noWaC* will be revised to this effect.

even though after document size filtering was applied our archive contained roughly twice as many documents, our final figures (number of tokens and number of documents) only amount to about half the size reported for the WaCky corpora (cf. table 1).

In particular, we observe that the most significant drop in size and in number of documents took place during the detection of duplicate and near-duplicate documents (drastically dropping from 11.4 million documents to 1.17 million documents after duplicate filtering). This indicates that, even if a huge number of documents in Bokmål Norwegian are present in the internet, a large portion of them must be machine generated content containing repeated n-grams that the duplicate removal tool successfully identifies and discards.[3]

These figures, although unexpected by us, may actually have a reasonable explanation. If we consider that Bokmål Norwegian has about 4.8 million potential content authors (assuming that every Norwegian inhabitant is able to produce web documents in Bokmål), and given that our final corpus contains 0.85 million documents, this means that we have so far sampled roughly one document every five potential writers: as good as it may sound, it is a highly unrealistic projection, and a great deal of noise and possibly also machine generated content must still be present in the corpus. The duplicate removal tools are only helping us understand that a speaker community can only produce a limited amount of linguistically relevant online content. We leave the interesting task of estimating the size of this content and its growth rate for further research. The Norwegian case, being a relatively small but highly developed information society, might prove to be a good starting point.

3.2 Scaling noWaC: how much Bokmål is there? How much did we get?

The question arises immediately. We want to know how representative our corpus is, in spite of the fact that we now know that it must still contain a great deal of noise and that a great deal of documents were plausibly not produced by human speakers.

To this effect, we applied the scaling factors methodology used by Kilgarrif (2007) to estimate the size of the Italian and German internet on the basis of the WaCky corpora. The method consists in comparing document hits for a sample of mid-frequency words in Google and in our corpus before and after duplicate removal. The method assumes that Google does indeed apply duplicate removal to some extent, though less drastically than we have. Cf. table 2 for some example figures.

From this document hit comparison, two scaling factors are extracted. The *scaling ratio* tells us how much smaller our corpus is compared to the Google index for Norwegian (including duplicates and non-running-text). The *duplicate ratio* gives us an idea of how much duplicated material was found in our archive.

Since we do not know exactly how much duplicate detection Google performs, we will multiply the duplicate ratio by a weight of 0.1, 0.25 and 0.5 (these weights, in turn, assume that Google discards 10 times less, 4 times less and half what our duplicate removal has done – the latter hypothesis is used by Kilgarriff 2007).

- Scaling ratio (average):
  Google frq. / noWaC raw frq. = 24.9
- Duplicate ratio (average):
  noWaC raw frq. / dedup. frq. = 7.8

We can then multiply the number of tokens in our final cleaned corpus by the scaling ratio and by the duplicate ratio (weighted) in order to obtain a rough estimate of how much Norwegian text is contained in the Google index. We can also estimate how much of this amount is present in *noWaC*. Cf. table 3.

Using exactly the same procedure as Kilgarrif (2007) leads us to conclude that *noWaC* should contain over **15%** of the Bokmål text indexed by Google. A much more restrictive estimate gives us about **3%**. More precise estimates are extremely difficult to make, and these results should be taken only as rough approximations. In any case, *noWaC* certainly is a reasonably representative web-corpus containing between 3% and 15% of all the currently indexed online Bokmål (Kilgarriff reports an estimate of 3% for German and 7% for Italian in the WaCky corpora).

[3]Although we are aware that the process of duplicate removal in *noWaC* must be refined further, constituting in itself an interesting research area.

	deWaC	*itWaC*	*ukWaC*	***noWaC***
N. of seed pairs	1,653	1,000	2,000	1,000
N. of seed URLs	8,626	5,231	6,528	6,891
Raw crawl size	398GB	379GB	351GB	**550GB**
Size after document size filter	20GB	19GB	19GB	22GB
N. of docs after document size filter	4.86M	4.43M	5.69M	11.4M
Size after near-duplicate filter	13GB	10GB	12GB	**5GB**
N. of docs after near-duplicate filter	1.75M	1.87M	2.69M	1.17M
N. of docs after lang-ID	–	–	–	**0.85M**
N. of tokens	1.27 Bn	1.58 Bn	1.91 Bn	**0.69 Bn**
N. of types	9.3M	3.6M	3.8M	6.0M

Table 1: Figure comparison of noWaC and the published WaCky corpora (German, Italian and British English data from Baroni et al. 2009)

Word	Google frq.	noWaC raw frq.	noWaC dedup. frq.
bilavgifter	33700	1637	314
mekanikk	82900	3266	661
musikkpris	16700	570	171

Table 2: Sample of Google and noWaC document frequencies before and after duplicate removal.

noWaC	Scaling ratio	Dup. ratio (weight)	Google estimate	% in noWaC
0.69 bn	24.9	0.78 (0.10)	21.8 bn	3.15%
		1.97 (0.25)	8.7 bn	7.89%
		3.94 (0.50)	4.3 bn	15.79%

Table 3: Estimating the size of the Bokmål Norwegian internet as indexed by Google in three different settings (method from Kilgarriff 2007)

4 Concluding remarks

Building large web-corpora for languages with a relatively small internet presence and with a limited speaker population presents problems and challenges that have not been found in previous work. In particular, the amount of data that can be collected with similar efforts is considerably smaller. In our experience, following as closely as possible the WaCky corpora methodology yielded a corpus that is roughly between one half and one third the size of the published comparable Italian, German and English corpora.

In any case, the experience has been very successful so far, and the first version of the *noWaC* corpus is about the same size than the largest currently available corpus of Norwegian (i.e. Norske Aviskorpus, 700 million tokens), and it has been created in just a minimal fraction of the time it took to build it.

Furthermore, the scaling experiments showed that *noWaC* is a very representative web-corpus containing a significant portion of all the online content in Bokmål Norwegian, in spite of our extremely drastic cleaning and filtering strategies.

There is clearly a great margin for improvement in almost every processing step we applied in this work. And there is clearly a lot to be done in order to qualitatively assess the created corpus. In the future, we intend to pursue this activity by carrying out an even greater crawling job in order to obtain a larger corpus, possibly containing over 1 billion tokens. Moreover, we shall reproduce this corpus creation process with the remaining two largest written languages of Norway, Nynorsk and North Sami. All of these resources will soon be publicly and freely available both for the general public and for the research community.

Acknowledgements

Building *noWaC* has been possible thanks to NOTUR advanced user support and assistance from the Research Computing Services group (Vitenskapelig Databehandling) at USIT, University of Oslo. Many thanks are due to Eros Zanchetta (U. of Bologna), Adriano Ferraresi (U. of Bologna) and Marco Baroni (U. of Trento) and two anonymous reviewers for their helpful comments and help.

References

M. Baroni and S. Bernardini. 2004. Bootcat: Bootstrapping corpora and terms from the web. In *Proceedings of LREC 2004*, pages 1313–1316, Lisbon. ELDA.

Marco Baroni, Silvia Bernardini, Adriano Ferraresi, and Eros Zanchetta. 2009. The wacky wide web: a collection of very large linguistically processed webcrawled corpora. *Language Resources and Evaluation*, 43(3):209–226, 09.

David Crystal. 2001. *Language and the Internet*. Cambridge University Press, Cambridge.

A. Ferraresi, E. Zanchetta, M. Baroni, and S. Bernardini. 2008. Introducing and evaluating ukWaC, a very large web-derived corpus of English. In *Proceedings of the WAC4 Workshop at LREC 2008*.

R. Ghani, R. Jones, and D. Mladenic. 2001. Mining the web to create minority language corpora. In *Proceedings of the tenth international conference on Information and knowledge management*, pages 279–286.

Johannessen J.B. Nøklestad A. Hagen, K. 2000. A constraint-based tagger for norwegian. *Odense Working Papers in Language and Communication*, 19(I).

Knut Hofland. 2000. A self-expanding corpus based on newspapers on the web. In *Proceedings of the Second International Language Resources and Evaluation Conference*, Paris. European Language Resources Association.

Adam Kilgarriff and Marco Baroni, editors. 2006. *Proceedings of the 2nd International Workshop on the Web as Corpus (EACL 2006 SIGWAC Workshop)*. Association for Computational Linguistics, East Stroudsburg, PA.

Adam Kilgarriff and Gregory Grefenstette. 2003. Introduction to the special issue on the web as corpus. *Computational Linguistics*, 29(3):333–348.

A. Kilgarriff. 2007. Googleology is bad science. *Computational Linguistics*, 33(1):147–151.

S. Sharoff. 2005. Open-source corpora: Using the net to fish for linguistic data. *International Journal of Corpus Linguistics*, (11):435–462.

Building a Korean Web Corpus for Analyzing Learner Language

Markus Dickinson
Indiana University
md7@indiana.edu

Ross Israel
Indiana University
raisrael@indiana.edu

Sun-Hee Lee
Wellesley College
slee6@wellesley.edu

Abstract

Post-positional particles are a significant source of errors for learners of Korean. Following methodology that has proven effective in handling English preposition errors, we are beginning the process of building a machine learner for particle error detection in L2 Korean writing. As a first step, however, we must acquire data, and thus we present a methodology for constructing large-scale corpora of Korean from the Web, exploring the feasibility of building corpora appropriate for a given topic and grammatical construction.

1 Introduction

Applications for assisting second language learners can be extremely useful when they make learners more aware of the non-native characteristics in their writing (Amaral and Meurers, 2006). Certain constructions, such as English prepositions, are difficult to characterize by grammar rules and thus are well-suited for machine learning approaches (Tetreault and Chodorow, 2008; De Felice and Pulman, 2008). Machine learning techniques are relatively portable to new languages, but new languages bring issues in terms of defining the language learning problem and in terms of acquiring appropriate data for training a machine learner.

We focus in this paper mainly on acquiring data for training a machine learning system. In particular, we are interested in situations where the task is constant—e.g., detecting grammatical errors in particles—but the domain might fluctuate. This is the case when a learner is asked to write an essay on a prompt (e.g., "What do you hope to do in life?"), and the prompts may vary by student, by semester, by instructor, etc. By isolating a particular domain, we can hope for greater degrees of accuracy; see, for example, the high accuracies for domain-specific grammar correction in Lee and Seneff (2006).

In this situation, we face the challenge of obtaining data which is appropriate both for: a) the topic the learners are writing about, and b) the linguistic construction of interest, i.e., containing enough relevant instances. In the ideal case, one could build a corpus directly for the types of learner data to analyze. Luckily, using the web as a data source can provide such specialized corpora (Baroni and Bernardini, 2004), in addition to larger, more general corpora (Sharoff, 2006). A crucial question, though, is how one goes about designing the right web corpus for analyzing learner language (see, e.g., Sharoff, 2006, for other contexts)

The area of difficulty for language learners which we focus on is that of Korean post-positional particles, akin to English prepositions (Lee et al., 2009; Ko et al., 2004). Korean is an important language to develop NLP techniques for (see, e.g., discussion in Dickinson et al., 2008), presenting a variety of features which are less prevalent in many Western languages, such as agglutinative morphology, a rich system of case marking, and relatively free word order. Obtaining data is important in the general case, as non-English languages tend to lack resources.

The correct usage of Korean particles relies on knowing lexical, syntactic, semantic, and discourse information (Lee et al., 2005), which makes this challenging for both learners and machines (cf. En-

Proceedings of the NAACL HLT 2010 Sixth Web as Corpus Workshop, pages 8–16,
Los Angeles, California, June 2010.

glish determiners in Han et al., 2006). The only other approach we know of, a parser-based one, had very low precision (Dickinson and Lee, 2009). A secondary contribution of this work is thus defining the particle error detection problem for a machine learner. It is important that the data represent the relationships between specific lexical items: in the comparable English case, for example, *interest* is usually found with *in*: ***interest*** *in/*with learning*.

The basic framework we employ is to train a machine learner on correct Korean data and then apply this system to learner text, to predict correct particle usage, which may differ from the learner's (cf. Tetreault and Chodorow, 2008). After describing the grammatical properties of particles in section 2, we turn to the general approach for obtaining relevant web data in section 3, reporting basic statistics for our corpora in section 4. We outline the machine learing set-up in section 5 and present initial results in section 6. These results help evaluate the best way to build specialized corpora for learner language.

2 Korean particles

Similar to English prepositions, Korean postpositional particles add specific meanings or grammatical functions to nominals. However, a particle cannot stand alone in Korean and needs to be attached to the preceding nominal. More importantly, particles indicate a wide range of linguistic functions, specifying grammatical functions, e.g., subject and object; semantic roles; and discourse functions. In (1), for instance, *ka* marks both the subject (function) and agent (semantic role), *eykey* the dative and beneficiary; and so forth.[1]

(1) Sumi-**ka** John-**eykey** chayk-**ul** ilhke-yo
Sumi-SBJ John-to book-OBJ read-polite
'Sumi reads a book to John.'

Particles can also combine with nominals to form modifiers, adding meanings of time, location, instrument, possession, and so forth, as shown in (2). Note in this case that the marker *ul/lul* has multiple uses.[2]

[1]We use the Yale Romanization scheme for writing Korean.
[2]*Ul/lul*, *un/nun*, etc. only differ phonologically.

(2) Sumi-ka John-**uy** cip-**eyse** ku-lul
Sumi-SBJ John-GEN house-LOC he-OBJ
twu sikan-**ul** kitaly-ess-ta.
two hours-OBJ wait-PAST-END
'Sumi waited for John for (the whole) two hours in his house.'

There are also particles associated with discourse meanings. For example, in (3) the topic marker *nun* is used to indicate old information or a discourse-salient entity, while the delimiter *to* implies that there is someone else Sumi likes. In this paper, we focus on syntactic/semantic particle usage for nominals, planning to extend to other cases in the future.

(3) Sumi-**nun** John-**to** cohahay.
Sumi-TOP John-also like
'Sumi likes John also.'

Due to these complex linguistic properties, particles are one of the most difficult topics for Korean language learners. In (4b), for instance, a learner might replace a subject particle (as in (4a)) with an object (Dickinson et al., 2008). Ko et al. (2004) report that particle errors were the second most frequent error in a study across different levels of Korean learners, and errors persist across levels (see also Lee et al., 2009).

(4) a. Sumi-*nun* chayk-*i* philyohay-yo
Sumi-TOP book-SBJ need-polite
'Sumi needs a book.'

b. *Sumi-nun chayk-**ul** philyohay-yo
Sumi-TOP book-OBJ need-polite
'Sumi needs a book.'

3 Approach

3.1 Acquiring training data

Due to the lexical relationships involved, machine learning has proven to be a good method for similar NLP problems like detecting errors in English preposition use. For example Tetreault and Chodorow (2008) use a maximum entropy classifier to build a model of correct preposition usage, with 7 million instances in their training set, and Lee and Knutsson (2008) use memory-based learning, with 10 million sentences in their training set. In expanding the paradigm to other languages, one problem is a dearth of data. It seems like a large data set is essential for moving forward.

For Korean, there are at least two corpora publicly available right now, the Penn Korean Treebank (Han et al., 2002), with hundreds of thousands of words, and the Sejong Corpus (a.k.a., The Korean National Corpus, The National Institute of Korean Language, 2007), with tens of millions of words. While we plan to include the Sejong corpus in future data, there are several reasons we pursue a different tack here. First, not every language has such resources, and we want to work towards a language-independent platform of data acquisition. Secondly, these corpora may not be a good model for the kinds of topics learners write about. For example, news texts are typically written more formally than learner writing. We want to explore ways to quickly build topic-specific corpora, and Web as Corpus (WaC) technology gives us tools to do this.[3]

3.2 Web as Corpus

To build web corpora, we use BootCat (Baroni and Bernardini, 2004). The process is an iterative algorithm to bootstrap corpora, starting with various seed terms. The procedure is as follows:

1. Select initial seeds (terms).
2. Combine seeds randomly.
3. Run Google/Yahoo queries.
4. Retrieve corpus.
5. Extract new seeds via corpus comparison.
6. Repeat steps #2-#5.

For non-ASCII languages, one needs to check the encoding of webpages in order to convert the text into UTF-8 for output, as has been done for, e.g., Japanese (e.g., Erjavec et al., 2008; Baroni and Ueyama, 2004). Using a UTF-8 version of BootCat, we modified the system by using a simple Perl module (`Encode::Guess`) to look for the EUC-KR encoding of most Korean webpages and switch it to UTF-8. The pages already in UTF-8 do not need to be changed.

3.3 Obtaining data

A crucial first step in constructing a web corpus is the selection of appropriate seed terms for constructing the corpus (e.g., Sharoff, 2006; Ueyama, 2006). In our particular case, this begins the question of how one builds a corpus which models native Korean and which provides appropriate data for the task of particle error detection. The data should be genre-appropriate and contain enough instances of the particles learners know and used in ways they are expected to use them (e.g., as temporal modifiers). A large corpus will likely satisfy these criteria, but has the potential to contain distracting information. In Korean, for example, less formal writing often omits particles, thereby biasing a machine learner towards under-guessing particles. Likewise, a topic with different typical arguments than the one in question may mislead the machine. We compare the effectiveness of corpora built in different ways in training a machine learner.

3.3.1 A general corpus

To construct a general corpus, we identify words likely to be in a learner's lexicon, using a list of 50 nouns for beginning Korean students for seeds. This includes basic vocabulary entries like the words for *mother, father, cat, dog, student, teacher*, etc.

3.3.2 A focused corpus

Since we often know what domain[4] learner essays are written about, we experiment with building a more topic-appropriate corpus. Accordingly, we select a smaller set of 10 seed terms based on the range of topics covered in our test corpus (see section 6.1), shown in figure 1. As a first trial, we select terms that are, like the aforementioned general corpus seeds, level-appropriate for learners of Korean.

han-kwuk 'Korea'	*sa-lam* 'person(s)'
han-kwuk-e 'Korean (lg.)'	*chin-kwu* 'friend'
kyey-cel 'season'	*ga-jok* 'family'
hayng-pok 'happiness'	*wun-tong* 'exercise'
ye-hayng 'travel'	*mo-im* 'gathering'

Figure 1: Seed terms for the focused corpus

3.3.3 A second focused corpus

There are several issues with the quality of data we obtain from our focused terms. From an initial observation (see section 4.1), the difficulty stems in part from the simplicity of the seed terms above,

[3] Tetreault and Chodorow (2009) use the web to derive learner errors; our work, however, tries to obtain correct data.

[4] By *domain*, we refer to the subject of a discourse.

leading to, for example, actual Korean learner data. To avoid some of this noise, we use a second set of seed terms, representing relevant words in the same domains, but of a more advanced nature, i.e., topic-appropriate words that may be outside of a typical learner's lexicon. Our hypothesis is that this is more likely to lead to native, quality Korean. For each one of the simple words above, we posit two more advanced words, as given in figure 2.

kyo-sa 'teacher'	*in-kan* 'human'
phyung-ka 'evaluation'	*cik-cang* 'workplace'
pen-yuk 'translation'	*wu-ceng* 'friendship'
mwun-hak 'literature'	*sin-loy* 'trust'
ci-kwu 'earth'	*cwu-min* 'resident'
swun-hwan 'circulation'	*kwan-kye* 'relation'
myeng-sang 'meditation'	*co-cik* 'organization'
phyeng-hwa 'peace'	*sik-i-yo-pep* 'diet'
tham-hem 'exploration'	*yen-mal* 'end of a year'
cwun-pi 'preparation'	*hayng-sa* 'event'

Figure 2: Seed terms for the second focused corpus

3.4 Web corpus parameters

One can create corpora of varying size and generality, by varying the parameters given to BootCaT. We examine three parameters here.

Number of seeds The first way to vary the type and size of corpus obtained is by varying the number of seed terms. The exact words given to BootCaT affect the domain of the resulting corpus, and utilizintg a larger set of seeds leads to more potential to create a bigger corpus. With 50 seed terms, for example, there are 19,600 possible 3-tuples, while there are only 120 possible 3-tuples for 10 seed terms, limiting the relevant pages that can be returned.

For the general (G) corpus, we use: G1) all 50 seed terms, G2) 5 sets of 10 seeds, the result of splitting the 50 seeds randomly into 5 buckets, and G3) 5 sets of 20 seeds, which expand the 10-seed sets in G2 by randomly selecting 10 other terms from the remaining 40 seeds. This breakdown into 11 sets (1 G1, 5 G2, 5 G3) allows us to examine the effect of using different amounts of general terms and facilitates easy comparison with the first focused corpus, which has only 10 seed terms.

For the first focused (F_1) corpus, we use: $F_1$1) the 10 seed terms, and $F_1$2) 5 sets of 20 seeds, obtained by combining $F_1$1 with each seed set from G2. This second group provides an opportunity to examine what happens when augmenting the focused seeds with more general terms; as such, this is a first step towards larger corpora which retain some focus. For the second focused corpus (F_2), we simply use the set of 20 seeds. We have 7 sets here (1 $F_1$1, 5 $F_1$2, 1 F_2), giving us a total of 18 seed term sets at this step.

Tuple length One can also experiment with tuple length in BootCat. The shorter the tuple, the more webpages that can potentially be returned, as short tuples are likely to occur in several pages (e.g., compare the number of pages that all of *person happiness season* occur in vs. *person happiness season exercise travel*). On the other hand, longer tuples are more likely truly relevant to the type of data of interest, more likely to lead to well-formed language. We experiment with tuples of different lengths, namely 3 and 5. With 2 different tuple lengths and 18 seed sets, we now have 36 sets.

Number of queries We still need to specify how many queries to send to the search engine. The maximum number is determined by the number of seeds and the tuple size. For 3-word tuples with 10 seed terms, for instance, there are 10 items to choose 3 objects from: $\binom{10}{3} = \frac{10!}{3!(10-3)!} = 120$ possibilities.

Using all combinations is feasible for small seed sets, but becomes infeasible for larger seed sets, e.g., $\binom{50}{5} = 2,118,760$ possibilities. To reduce this, we opt for the following: for 3-word tuples, we generate 120 queries for all cases and 240 queries for the conditions with 20 and 50 seeds. Similarly, for 5-word tuples, we generate the maximum 252 queries with 10 seeds, and both 252 and 504 for the other conditions. With the previous 36 sets (12 of which have 10 seed terms), evenly split between 3 and 5-word tuples, we now have 60 total corpora, as in table 1.

		# of seeds					
tuple	# of	General			F_1		F_2
len.	queries	10	20	50	10	20	20
3	120	5	5	1	1	5	1
	240	n/a	5	1	n/a	5	1
5	252	5	5	1	1	5	1
	504	n/a	5	1	n/a	5	1

Table 1: Number of corpora based on parameters

Other possibilities There are other ways to increase the size of a web corpus using BootCaT. First, one can increase the number of returned pages for a particular query. We set the limit at 20, as anything higher will more likely result in non-relevant data for the focused corpora and/or duplicate documents.

Secondly, one can perform iterations of searching, extracting new seed terms with every iteration. Again, the concern is that by iterating away from the initial seeds, a corpus could begin to lose focus. We are considering both extensions for the future.

Language check One other constraint we use is to specify the particular language of interest, namely that we want Korean pages. This parameter is set using the language option when collecting URLs. We note that a fair amount of English, Chinese, and Japanese appears in these pages, and we are currently developing our own Korean filter.

4 Corpus statistics

To gauge the properties of size, genre, and degree of particle usage in the corpora, independent of application, basic statistics of the different web corpora are given in table 2, where we average over multiple corpora for conditions with 5 corpora.[5]

There are a few points to understand in the table. First, it is hard to count true words in Korean, as compounds are frequent, and particles have a debatable status. From a theory-neutral perspective, we count *ejel*s, which are tokens occurring between white spaces. Secondly, we need to know about the number of particles and number of nominals, i.e., words which could potentially bear particles, as our machine learning paradigm considers any nominal a test case for possible particle attachment. We use a POS tagger (Han and Palmer, 2004) for this.

Some significant trends emerge when comparing the corpora in the table. First of all, longer queries (length 5) result in not only more returned unique webpages, but also longer webpages on average than shorter queries (length 3). This effect is most dramatic for the F_2 corpora. The F_2 corpora also exhibit a higher ratio of particles to nominals than the other web corpora, which means there will be more positive examples in the training data for the machine learner based on the F_2 corpora.

[5]For the 252 5-tuple 20 seed General corpora, we average over four corpora, due to POS tagging failure on the fifth corpus.

4.1 Qualitative evaluation

In tandem with the basic statistics, it is also important to gauge the quality of the Korean data from a more qualitative perspective. Thus, we examined the 120 3-tuple F_1 corpus and discovered a number of problems with the data.

First, there are issues concerning collecting data which is not pure Korean. We find data extracted from Chinese travel sites, where there is a mixture of non-standard foreign words and unnatural-sounding translated words in Korean. Ironically, we also find learner data of Korean in our search for correct Korean data. Secondly, there are topics which, while exhibiting valid forms of Korean, are too far afield from what we expect learners to know, including religious sites with rare expressions; poems, which commonly drop particles; gambling sites; and so forth. Finally, there are cases of ungrammatical uses of Korean, which are used in specific contexts not appropriate for our purposes. These include newspaper titles, lists of personal names and addresses, and incomplete phrases from advertisements and chats. In these cases, we tend to find less particles.

Based on these properties, we developed the aforementioned second focused corpus with more advanced Korean words and examined the 240 3-tuple F_2 corpus. The F_2 seeds allow us to capture a greater percentage of well-formed data, namely data from news articles, encyclopedic texts, and blogs about more serious topics such as politics, literature, and economics. While some of this data might be above learners' heads, it is, for the most part, well-formed native-like Korean. Also, the inclusion of learner data has been dramatically reduced. However, some of the same problems from the F_1 corpus persist, namely the inclusion of poetry, newspaper titles, religious text, and non-Korean data.

Based on this qualitative analysis, it is clear that we need to filter out more data than is currently being filtered, in order to obtain valid Korean of a type which uses a sufficient number of particles in grammatical ways. In the future, we plan on restricting the genre, filtering based on the number of rare words (e.g., religious words), and using a trigram language model to check the validity.

Corpus	Seeds	Len.	Queries	URLs	Ejel Total	Ejel Avg.	Particles Total	Particles Avg.	Nominals Total	Nominals Avg.
Gen.	10	3	120	1096.2	1,140,394.6	1044.8	363,145.6	331.5	915,025	838.7
		5	252	1388.2	2,430,346.4	1779.9	839,005.8	618.9	1,929,266.0	1415.3
	20	3	120	1375.2	1,671,549.2	1222.1	540,918	394.9	1,350,976.6	988.6
		3	240	2492.4	2,735,201.6	1099.4	889,089	357.3	2,195,703	882.4
		5	252	1989.6	4,533,642.4	2356	1,359,137.2	724.5	3,180,560.6	1701.5
		5	504	3487	7,463,776	2193.5	2,515,235.8	741.6	5,795,455.8	1709.7
	50	3	120	1533	1,720,261	1122.1	584,065	380.9	1,339,308	873.6
		3	240	2868	3,170,043	1105.3	1,049,975	366.1	2,506,995	874.1
		5	252	1899.5	4,380,684.2	2397.6	1,501,358.7	821.5	3,523,746.2	1934.6
		5	504	5636	5,735,859	1017.7	1,773,596	314.6	4,448,815	789.3
F_1	10	3	120	1315	628,819	478.1	172,415	131.1	510,620	388.3
		5	252	1577	1,364,885	865.4	436,985	277.1	1,069,898	678.4
	20	3	120	1462.6	1,093,772.4	747.7	331,457.8	226.8	885,157.2	604.9
			240	2637.2	1,962,741.8	745.2	595,570.6	226.1	1,585,730.4	602.1
		5	252	2757.6	2,015,077.8	730.8	616,163.8	223.4	1,621,306.2	588
			504	4734	3,093,140.4	652.9	754,610	159.8	1,993,104.4	422.1
F_2	20	3	120	1417	1,054,925	744.5	358,297	252.9	829,416	585.3
			240	2769	1,898,383	685.6	655,757	236.8	1,469,623	530.7
		5	252	1727	4,510,742	2611.9	1,348,240	780.7	2,790,667	1615.9
			504	2680	6,916,574	2580.8	2,077,171	775.1	4,380,571	1634.5

Table 2: Basic statistics of different web corpora

Note that one might consider building even larger corpora from the start and using the filtering step to winnow down the corpus for a particular application, such as particle error detection. However, while removing ungrammatical Korean is a process of removing noise, identifying whether a corpus is about traveling, for example, is a content-based decision. Given that this is what a search engine is designed to do, we prefer filtering based only on grammatical and genre properties.

5 Classification

We describe the classification paradigm used to determine how effective each corpus is for detecting correct particle usage; evaluation is in section 6.

5.1 Machine learning paradigm

Based on the parallel between Korean particles and English prepositions, we use preposition error detection as a starting point for developing a classifier. For prepositions, Tetreault and Chodorow (2008) extract 25 features to guess the correct preposition (out of 34 selected prepositions), including features capturing the lexical and grammatical context (e.g., the words and POS tags in a two-word window around the preposition) and features capturing various relevant selectional properties (e.g., the head verb and noun of the preceding VP and NP).

We are currently using TiMBL (Daelemans et al., 2007) for development purposes, as it provides a range of options for testing. Given that learner data needs to be processed instantaneously and that memory-based learning can take a long time to classify, we will revisit this choice in the future.

5.2 Defining features

5.2.1 Relevant properties of Korean

As discussed in section 2, Korean has major differences from English, leading to different features. First, the base word order of Korean is SOV, which means that the following verb and following noun could determine how the current word functions. However, since Korean allows for freer word order than English, we do not want to completely disregard the previous noun or verb, either.

Secondly, the composition of words is different than English. Words contain a stem and an arbitrary number of suffixes, which may be derivational morphemes as well as particles, meaning that we must consider sub-word features, i.e., segment words into their component morphemes.

Finally, particles have more functions than prepositions, requiring a potentially richer space of features. Case marking, for example, is even more dependent upon the word's grammatical function in a sentence. In order to ensure that our system can correctly handle all of the typical relations between words without failing on less frequent constructions, we need (large amounts of) appropriate data.

5.2.2 Feature set

To begin with, we segment and POS tag the text, using a hybrid (trigram + rule-based) morphological tagger for Korean (Han and Palmer, 2004). This segmentation phase means that we can define subword features and isolate the particles in question. For our features, we break each word into: a) its stem and b) its combined affixes (excluding particles), and each of these components has its own POS, possibly a combined tag (e.g., EPF+EFN), with tags from the Penn Korean Treebank (Han et al., 2002).

The feature vector uses a five word window that includes the target word and two words on either side for context. Each word is broken down into four features: stem, affixes, stem_POS, and affixes_POS. Given the importance of surrounding noun and verbs for attachment in Korean, we have features for the preceding as well as the following noun and verb. For the noun/verb features, only the stem is used, as this is largely a semantically-based property.

In terms of defining a class, if the target word's affixes contain a particle, it is removed and used as the basis for the class; otherwise the class is NONE. We also remove particles in the context affixes, as we cannot rely on surrounding learner particles.

As an example, consider predicting the particle for the word *Yenge* ('English') in (5a). We generate the instance in (5b). The first five lines refer to the previous two words, the target word, and the following two words, each split into stem and suffixes along with their POS tags, and with particles removed. The sixth line contains the stems of the preceding and following noun and verb, and finally, there is the class (YES/NO).

(5) a. Mikwuk-*eyse* sal-*myense* Yenge-*man-ul* cip-*eyse* ss-*ess-eyo*.
America-in live-while English-only-OBJ home-at use-Past-Decl
'While living in America, (I/she/he) used only English at home.'

b. Mikwuk NPR NONE NONE
sal VV myense ECS
Yenge NPR NONE NONE
cip NNC NONE NONE
ss VV ess+eyo EPF+EFN
sal Mikwuk ss cip
YES

For the purposes of evaluating the different corpora, we keep the task simple and only guess YES or NO for the existence of a particle. We envision this as a first pass, where the specific particle can be guessed later. This is also a practical task, in that learners can benefit from accurate feedback on knowing whether or not a particle is needed.

6 Evaluation

We evaluate the web corpora for the task of predicting particle usage, after describing the test corpus.

6.1 Learner Corpus

To evaluate, we use a corpus of learner Korean made up of essays from college students (Lee et al., 2009). The corpus is divided according to student level (beginner, intermediate) and student background (heritage, non-heritage),[6] and is hand-annotated for particle errors. We expect beginners to be less accurate than intermediates and non-heritage less accurate than heritage learners. To pick a middle ground, the current research has been conducted on non-heritage intermediate learners. The test corpus covers a range of common language classroom topics such as Korean language, Korea, friends, family, and traveling.

We run our system on raw learner data, i.e, unsegmented and with spelling and spacing errors included. As mentioned in section 5.2.2, we use a POS tagger to segment the words into morphemes, a crucial step for particle error detection.[7]

[6] Heritage learners have had exposure to Korean at a young age, such as growing up with Korean spoken at home.

[7] In the case of segmentation errors, we cannot possibly get the particle correct. We are currently investigating this issue.

	Seeds	Len.	Quer.	P	R	F
Gen.	10	3	120	81.54%	76.21%	78.77%
		5	252	82.98%	77.77%	80.28%
	20	3	120	81.56%	77.26%	79.33%
		3	240	82.89%	78.37%	80.55%
		5	252	83.79%	78.17%	80.87%
		5	504	84.30%	79.44%	81.79%
	50	3	120	82.97%	77.97%	80.39%
		3	240	83.62%	80.46%	82.00%
		5	252	82.57%	78.45%	80.44%
		5	504	84.25%	78.69%	81.36%
F_1	10	3	120	81.41%	74.67%	77.88%
		5	252	83.82%	77.09%	80.30%
	20	3	120	82.23%	76.40%	79.20%
			240	82.57%	77.19%	79.78%
		5	252	83.62%	77.97%	80.68%
			504	81.86%	75.88%	78.73%
F_2	20	3	120	81.63%	76.44%	78.93%
			240	82.57%	78.45%	80.44%
		5	252	84.21%	80.62%	82.37%
			504	83.87%	81.51%	82.67%

Table 3: Results of guessing particle existence, training with different corpora

The non-heritage intermediate (NHI) corpus gives us 3198 words, with 1288 particles and 1836 nominals. That is, about 70% of the nominals in the learner corpus are followed by a particle. This is a much higher average than in the 252 5-tuple F_2 corpus, which exhibits the highest average of all of the web corpora at about 48% ($\frac{781}{1616}$; see table 2).

6.2 Results

We use the default settings for TiMBL for all the results we report here. Though we have obtained 4-5% higher F-scores using different settings, the comparisons between corpora are the important measure for the current task. The results are given in table 3.

The best results were achieved when training on the 5-tuple F_2 corpora, leading to F-scores of 82.37% and 82.67% for the 252 tuple and 504 tuple corpora, respectively. This finding reinforces our hypothesis that more advanced seed terms result in more reliable Korean data, while staying within the domain of the test corpus. Both longer tuple lengths and greater amounts of queries have an effect on the reliability of the resulting corpora. Specificaly, 5-tuple corpora produce better results than similar 3-tuple corpora, and corpora with double the amount of queries of n-length perform better than smaller comparable corpora. Although larger corpora tend to do better, it is important to note that there is not a clear relationship. The general 50/5/252 corpus, for instance, is similarly-sized to the F_2 focused 20/5/252 corpus, with over 4 million ejels (see table 2). The focused corpus—based on fewer yet more relevant seed terms—has 2% better F-score.

7 Summary and Outlook

In this paper, we have examined different ways to build web corpora for analyzing learner language to support the detection of errors in Korean particles. This type of investigation is most useful for lesser-resourced languages, where the error detection task stays constant, but the topic changes frequently. In order to develop a framework for testing web corpora, we have also begun developing a machine learning system for detecting particle errors.

The current web data, as we have demonstrated, is not perfect, and thus we need to continue improving that. One approach will be to filter out clearly non-Korean data, as suggested in section 4.1. We may also explore instance sampling (e.g., Wunsch et al., 2009) to remove many of the non-particle nominal (negative) instances, which will reduce the difference between the ratios of negative-to-positive instances of the web and learner corpora. We still feel that there is room for improvement in our seed term selection, and plan on constructing specific web corpora for each topic covered in the learner corpus. We will also consider adding currently available corpora, such as the Sejong Corpus (The National Institute of Korean Language, 2007), to our web data.

With better data, we can work on improving the machine learning system. This includes optimizing the set of features, the parameter settings, and the choice of machine learning algorithm. Once the system has been optimized, we will need to test the results on a wider range of learner data.

Acknowledgments

We would like to thank Marco Baroni and Jan Pomikálek for kindly providing a UTF-8 version of BootCat; Chong Min Lee for help with the POS tagger, provided by Chung-Hye Han; and Joel Tetreault for useful discussion.

References

Amaral, Luiz and Detmar Meurers (2006). Where does ICALL Fit into Foreign Language Teaching? Talk given at CALICO Conference. May 19, 2006. University of Hawaii.

Baroni, Marco and Silvia Bernardini (2004). BootCaT: Bootstrapping Corpora and Terms from the Web. In *Proceedings of LREC 2004*. pp. 1313–1316.

Baroni, Marco and Motoko Ueyama (2004). Retrieving Japanese specialized terms and corpora from the World Wide Web. In *Proceedings of KONVENS 2004*.

Daelemans, Walter, Jakub Zavrel, Ko van der Sloot, Antal van den Bosch, Timbl Tilburg and Memory based Learner (2007). TiMBL: Tilburg Memory-Based Learner - version 6.1 - Reference Guide.

De Felice, Rachele and Stephen Pulman (2008). A classifier-baed approach to preposition and determiner error correction in L2 English. In *Proceedings of COLING-08*. Manchester.

Dickinson, Markus, Soojeong Eom, Yunkyoung Kang, Chong Min Lee and Rebecca Sachs (2008). A Balancing Act: How can intelligent computer-generated feedback be provided in learner-to-learner interactions. *Computer Assisted Language Learning* 21(5), 369–382.

Dickinson, Markus and Chong Min Lee (2009). Modifying Corpus Annotation to Support the Analysis of Learner Language. *CALICO Journal* 26(3).

Erjavec, Irena Srdanovič, Tomaz Erjavec and Adam Kilgarriff (2008). A Web Corpus and Word Sketches for Japanese. *Information and Media Technologies* 3(3), 529–551.

Han, Chung-Hye, Na-Rare Han, Eon-Suk Ko and Martha Palmer (2002). Development and Evaluation of a Korean Treebank and its Application to NLP. In *Proceedings of LREC-02*.

Han, Chung-Hye and Martha Palmer (2004). A Morphological Tagger for Korean: Statistical Tagging Combined with Corpus-Based Morphological Rule Application. *Machine Translation* 18(4), 275–297.

Han, Na-Rae, Martin Chodorow and Claudia Leacock (2006). Detecting Errors in English Article Usage by Non-Native Speakers. *Natural Language Engineering* 12(2).

Ko, S., M. Kim, J. Kim, S. Seo, H. Chung and S. Han (2004). *An analysis of Korean learner corpora and errors*. Hanguk Publishing Co.

Lee, John and Ola Knutsson (2008). The Role of PP Attachment in Preposition Generation. In *Proceedings of CICLing 2008*. Haifa, Israel.

Lee, John and Stephanie Seneff (2006). Automatic Grammar Correction for Second-Language Learners. In *INTERSPEECH 2006*. Pittsburgh, pp. 1978–1981.

Lee, Sun-Hee, Donna K. Byron and Seok Bae Jang (2005). Why is Zero Marking Important in Korean? In *Proceedings of IJCNLP-05*. Jeju Island, Korea.

Lee, Sun-Hee, Seok Bae Jang and Sang kyu Seo (2009). Annotation of Korean Learner Corpora for Particle Error Detection. *CALICO Journal* 26(3).

Sharoff, Serge (2006). Creating General-Purpose Corpora Using Automated Search Engine Queries. In *WaCky! Working papers on the Web as Corpus. Gedit*.

Tetreault, Joel and Martin Chodorow (2008). The Ups and Downs of Preposition Error Detection in ESL Writing. In *Proceedings of COLING-08*. Manchester.

Tetreault, Joel and Martin Chodorow (2009). Examining the Use of Region Web Counts for ESL Error Detection. In *Web as Corpus Workshop (WAC-5)*. San Sebastian, Spain.

The National Institute of Korean Language (2007). The Sejong Corpus.

Ueyama, Motoko (2006). Evaluation of Japanese Web-based Reference Corpora: Effects of Seed Selection and Time Interval. In *WaCky! Working papers on the Web as Corpus. Gedit*.

Wunsch, Holger, Sandra Kübler and Rachael Cantrell (2009). Instance Sampling Methods for Pronoun Resolution. In *Proceedings of RANLP 2009*. Borovets, Bulgaria.

Sketching Techniques for Large Scale NLP

Amit Goyal, Jagadeesh Jagarlamudi, Hal Daumé III, and Suresh Venkatasubramanian
University of Utah, School of Computing
{amitg, jags, hal, suresh}@cs.utah.edu

Abstract

In this paper, we address the challenges posed by large amounts of text data by exploiting the power of hashing in the context of streaming data. We explore sketch techniques, especially the Count-Min Sketch, which approximates the frequency of a word pair in the corpus without explicitly storing the word pairs themselves. We use the idea of a conservative update with the Count-Min Sketch to reduce the average relative error of its approximate counts by a factor of two. We show that it is possible to store all words and word pairs counts computed from 37 GB of web data in just 2 billion counters (8 GB RAM). The number of these counters is up to 30 times less than the stream size which is a big memory and space gain. In Semantic Orientation experiments, the PMI scores computed from 2 billion counters are as effective as exact PMI scores.

1 Introduction

Approaches to solve NLP problems (Brants et al., 2007; Turney, 2008; Ravichandran et al., 2005) always benefited from having large amounts of data. In some cases (Turney and Littman, 2002; Patwardhan and Riloff, 2006), researchers attempted to use the evidence gathered from web via search engines to solve the problems. But the commercial search engines limit the number of automatic requests on a daily basis for various reasons such as to avoid fraud and computational overhead. Though we can crawl the data and save it on disk, most of the current approaches employ data structures that reside in main memory and thus do not scale well to huge corpora.

Fig. 1 helps us understand the seriousness of the situation. It plots the number of unique words/word pairs versus the total number of words in a corpus of size 577 MB. Note that the plot is in log-log scale. This 78 million word corpus generates 63 thousand unique words and 118 million unique word pairs. As expected, the rapid increase in number of unique word pairs is much larger than the increase in number of words. Hence, it shows that it is computationally infeasible to compute counts of all word pairs with a giant corpora using conventional main memory of 8 GB.

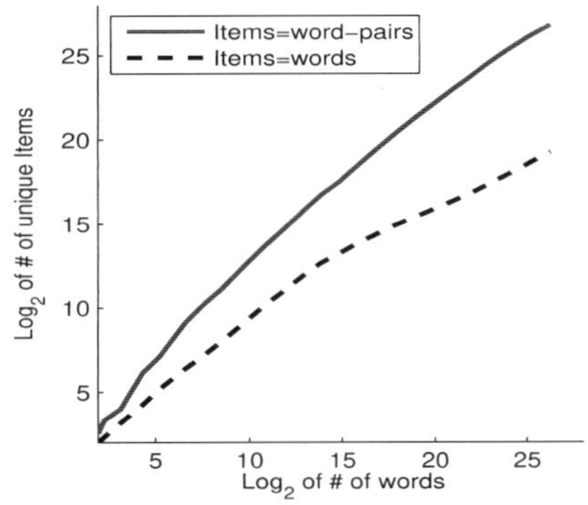

Figure 1: Token Type Curve

Storing only the 118 million unique word pairs in this corpus require 1.9 GB of disk space. This space can be saved by avoiding storing the word pair itself. As a trade-off we are willing to tolerate a small amount of error in the frequency of each word pair. In this paper, we explore sketch techniques, especially the Count-Min Sketch, which approximates the frequency of a word pair in the corpus without explicitly storing the word pairs themselves. It turns out that, in this technique, both updating (adding a new word pair or increasing the frequency of existing word pair) and querying (finding the frequency of a given word pair) are very efficient and can be done in constant time[1].

Counts stored in the CM Sketch can be used to compute various word-association measures like

[1]depend only on one of the user chosen parameters

Proceedings of the NAACL HLT 2010 Sixth Web as Corpus Workshop, pages 17–25,
Los Angeles, California, June 2010.

Pointwise Mutual Information (PMI), and Log-Likelihood ratio. These association scores are useful for other NLP applications like word sense disambiguation, speech and character recognition, and computing semantic orientation of a word. In our work, we use computing semantic orientation of a word using PMI as a canonical task to show the effectiveness of CM Sketch for computing association scores.

In our attempt to advocate the Count-Min sketch to store the frequency of keys (words or word pairs) for NLP applications, we perform both intrinsic and extrinsic evaluations. In our intrinsic evaluation, first we show that low-frequent items are more prone to errors. Second, we show that computing approximate PMI scores from these counts can give the same ranking as Exact PMI. However, we need counters linear in size of stream to achieve that. We use these approximate PMI scores in our extrinsic evaluation of computing semantic orientation. Here, we show that we do not need counters linear in size of stream to perform as good as Exact PMI. In our experiments, by using only 2 billion counters (8GB RAM) we get the same accuracy as for exact PMI scores. The number of these counters is up to 30 times less than the stream size which is a big memory and space gain without any loss of accuracy.

2 Background

2.1 Large Scale NLP problems

Use of large data in the NLP community is not new. A corpus of roughly 1.6 Terawords was used by Agirre et al. (2009) to compute pairwise similarities of the words in the test sets using the MapReduce infrastructure on $2,000$ cores. Pantel et al. (2009) computed similarity between 500 million terms in the MapReduce framework over a 200 billion words in 50 hours using 200 quad-core nodes. The inaccessibility of clusters for every one has attracted the NLP community to use streaming, randomized, approximate and sampling algorithms to handle large amounts of data.

A randomized data structure called Bloom filter was used to construct space efficient language models (Talbot and Osborne, 2007) for Statistical Machine Translation (SMT). Recently, the *streaming algorithm* paradigm has been used to provide memory and space-efficient platform to deal with terabytes of data. For example, We (Goyal et al., 2009) pose language modeling as a problem of finding frequent items in a stream of data and show its effectiveness in SMT. Subsequently, (Levenberg and Osborne, 2009) proposed a randomized language model to efficiently deal with unbounded text streams. In (Van Durme and Lall, 2009b), authors extend Talbot Osborne Morris Bloom (TOMB) (Van Durme and Lall, 2009a) Counter to find the highly ranked k PMI response words given a cue word. The idea of TOMB is similar to CM Sketch. TOMB can also be used to store word pairs and further compute PMI scores. However, we advocate CM Sketch as it is a very simple algorithm with strong guarantees and good properties (see Section 3).

2.2 Sketch Techniques

A sketch is a summary data structure that is used to store streaming data in a memory efficient manner. These techniques generally work on an input stream, i.e. they process the input in one direction, say from left to right, without going backwards. The main advantage of these techniques is that they require storage which is significantly smaller than the input stream length. For typical algorithms, the working storage is sublinear in N, i.e. of the order of $\log^k N$, where N is the input size and k is some constant which is not explicitly chosen by the algorithm but it is an artifact of it.. Sketch based methods use hashing to map items in the streaming data onto a small-space sketch vector that can be easily updated and queried. It turns out that both updating and querying on this sketch vector requires only a constant time per operation.

Streaming algorithms were first developed in the early 80s, but gained in popularity in the late 90s as researchers first realized the challenges of dealing with massive data sets. A good survey of the model and core challenges can be found in (Muthukrishnan, 2005). There has been considerable work on coming up with different sketch techniques (Charikar et al., 2002; Cormode and Muthukrishnan, 2004; Li and Church, 2007). A survey by (Rusu and Dobra, 2007; Cormode and Hadjieleftheriou, 2008) comprehensively reviews the literature.

3 Count-Min Sketch

The Count-Min Sketch (Cormode and Muthukrishnan, 2004) is a compact summary data structure used to store the frequencies of all items in the input stream. The sketch allows fundamental queries on the data stream such as point, range and inner product queries to be approximately answered very quickly. It can also be applied to solve the finding frequent items problem (Manku and Motwani, 2002) in a data stream. In this paper, we are only interested in point queries. The aim of a point query is to estimate the count of an item in the input stream. For other details, the reader is referred to (Cormode and Muthukrishnan, 2004).

Given an input stream of word pairs of length N and user chosen parameters δ and ϵ, the algorithm stores the frequencies of all the word pairs with the following guarantees:

- All reported frequencies are within the true frequencies by at most ϵN with a probability of at least δ.
- The space used by the algorithm is $O(\frac{1}{\epsilon}\log\frac{1}{\delta})$.
- Constant time of O(log($\frac{1}{\delta}$)) per each update and query operation.

3.1 CM Data Structure

A Count-Min Sketch with parameters (ϵ,δ) is represented by a two-dimensional array with width w and depth d :

$$\begin{bmatrix} \text{sketch[1,1]} & \cdots & \text{sketch[1,w]} \\ \vdots & \ddots & \vdots \\ \text{sketch[d,1]} & \cdots & \text{sketch[d,w]} \end{bmatrix}$$

Among the user chosen parameters, ϵ controls the amount of tolerable error in the returned count and δ controls the probability with which the returned count is not within the accepted error. These values of ϵ and δ determine the width and depth of the two-dimensional array respectively. To achieve the guarantees mentioned in the previous section, we set w=$\frac{2}{\epsilon}$ and d=log($\frac{1}{\delta}$). The depth d denotes the number of pairwise-independent hash functions employed by the algorithm and there exists an one-to-one correspondence between the rows and the set of hash functions. Each of these hash functions h_k:$\{1 \ldots N\} \rightarrow \{1 \ldots w\}$ $(1 \leq k \leq d)$ takes an item from the input stream and maps it into a counter indexed by the corresponding hash function. For example, $h_2(w) = 10$ indicates that the word pair w is mapped to the 10th position in the second row of the sketch array. These d hash functions are chosen uniformly at random from a pairwise-independent family.

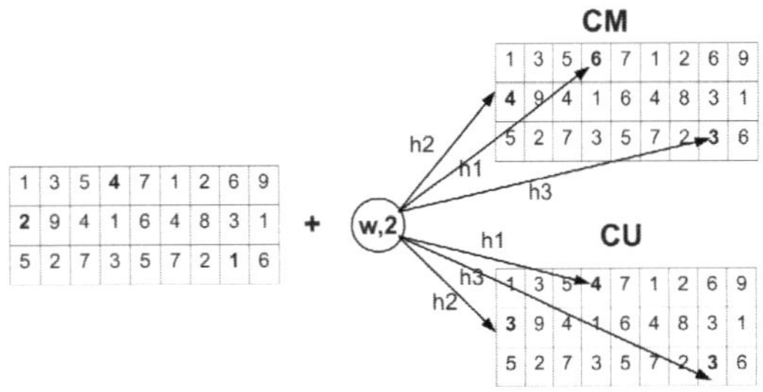

Figure 2: Update Procedure for CM sketch and conservative update (CU)

Initially the entire sketch array is initialized with zeros.

Update Procedure: When a new item (w,c) arrives, where w is a word pair and c is its count[2], one counter in each row, as decided by its corresponding hash function, is updated by c. Formally, $\forall 1 \leq k \leq d$

$$\text{sketch[k,}h_k(w)\text{]} \leftarrow \text{sketch[k,}h_k(w)\text{]} + c$$

This process is illustrated in Fig. 2 CM. The item (w,2) arrives and gets mapped to three positions, corresponding to the three hash functions. Their counts before update were (4,2,1) and after update they become (6,4,3). Note that, since we are using a hash to map a word into an index, a collision can occur and multiple word pairs may get mapped to the same counter in any given row. Because of this, the values stored by the d counters for a given word pair tend to differ.

Query Procedure: The querying involves finding the frequency of a given item in the input stream. Since multiple word pairs can get mapped into same counter and the observation that the counts of items are positive, the frequency stored by each counter is an overestimate of the true count. So in answering the point query, we consider all the positions indexed by the hash functions for the given word pair and return the minimum of all these values. The answer to Query(w) is:

$$\hat{c} = min_k \text{ sketch[k,}h_k(w)\text{]}$$

Note that, instead of positive counts if we had negative counts as well then the algorithm returns the median of all the counts and the bounds we discussed in Sec. 3 vary. In Fig. 2 CM, for the word pair w it takes the minimum over (6,4,3) and returns 3 as the count of word pair w.

[2]In our setting, c is always 1. However, in other NLP problem, word pairs can be weighted according to recency.

Both update and query procedures involve evaluating d hash functions and a linear scan of all the values in those indices and hence both these procedures are linear in the number of hash functions. Hence both these steps require $O(\log(\frac{1}{\delta}))$ time. In our experiments (see Section 4.2), we found that a small number of hash functions are sufficient and we use d=3. Hence, the update and query operations take only a constant time. The space used by the algorithm is the size of the array i.e. wd counters, where w is the width of each row.

3.2 Properties

Apart from the advantages of being space efficient, and having constant update and constant querying time, the Count-Min sketch has also other advantages that makes it an attractive choice for NLP applications.

- Linearity: given two sketches s_1 and s_2 computed (using the same parameters w and d) over different input streams, the sketch of the combined data stream can be easily obtained by adding the individual sketches in O($\frac{1}{\epsilon}\log\frac{1}{\delta}$) time which is independent of the stream size.

- The linearity is especially attractive because, it allows the individual sketches to be computed independent of each other. Which means that it is easy to implement it in distributed setting, where each machine computes the sketch over a sub set of corpus.

- This technique also extends to allow the deletion of items. In this case, to answer a point query, we should return the median of all the values instead of the minimum value.

3.3 Conservative Update

Estan and Varghese introduce the idea of conservative update (Estan and Varghese, 2002) in the context of networking. This can easily be used with CM Sketch to further improve the estimate of a point query. To update an item, word pair, w with frequency c, we first compute the frequency $\hat{c}$ of this item from the existing data structure and the counts are updated according to: $\forall 1 \leq k \leq d$

$$\text{sketch[k,}h_k(w)\text{]} \leftarrow \max\{\text{sketch[k,}h_k(w)\text{]}, \hat{c} + \text{c}\}$$

The intuition is that, since the point query returns the minimum of all the d values, we will update a counter only if it is necessary as indicated by the above equation. Though this is a heuristic, it avoids the unnecessary updates of counter values and thus reduces the error.

The process is also illustrated in Fig. 2CU. When an item "w" with a frequency of 2 arrives in the stream, it gets mapped into three positions in the sketch data structure. Their counts before update were (4,2,1) and the frequency of the item is 1 (the minimum of all the three values). In this particular case, the update rule says that increase the counter value only if its updated value is less than $\hat{c} + 2 = 3$. As a result, the values in these counters after the update become (4,3,3).

However, if the value in any of the counters is already greater than 3 e.g. 4, we cannot attempt to correct it by decreasing, as it could contain the count for other items hashed at that position. Therefore, in this case, for the first counter we leave the value 4 unchanged. The query procedure remains the same as in the previous case. In our experiments, we found that employing the conservative update reduces the Average Relative Error (ARE) of these counts approximately by a factor of 2. (see Section 4.2). But unfortunately, this update prevents deletions and items with negative updates cannot be processed[3].

4 Intrinsic Evaluations

To show the effectiveness of the Count-Min sketch in the context of NLP, we perform intrinsic evaluations. The intrinsic evaluations are designed to measure the error in the approximate counts returned by CMS compared to their true counts. By keeping the total size of the data structure fixed, we study the error by varying the width and the depth of the data structure to find the best setting of the parameters for textual data sets. We show that using conservative update (CU) further improves the quality of counts over CM sketch.

4.1 Corpus Statistics

Gigaword corpus (Graff, 2003) and a copy of web crawled by (Ravichandran et al., 2005) are used to compute counts of words and word pairs. For both the corpora, we split the text into sentences, tokenize and convert into lower-case. We generate words and word pairs (items) over a sliding window of size 14. Unlike previous work (Van Durme

[3]Here, we are only interested in the insertion case.

Corpus	Sub set	Giga word	50% Web	100% Web
Size GB	.15	6.2	15	31
# of sentences (Million)	2.03	60.30	342.68	686.63
# of words (Million)	19.25	858.92	2122.47	4325.03
Stream Size 10 (Billion)	0.25	19.25	18.63	39.05
Stream Size 14 (Billion)	0.23	25.94	18.79	40.00

Table 1: Corpus Description

and Lall, 2009b) which assumes exact frequencies for words, we store frequencies of both the words and word pairs in the CM sketch[4]. Hence, the stream size in our case is the total number of words and word pairs in a corpus. Table 1 gives the characteristics of the corpora.

Since, it is not possible to compute exact frequencies of all word pairs using conventional main memory of 8 GB from a large corpus, we use a subset of 2 million sentences (Subset) from Gigaword corpus for our intrinsic evaluation. We store the counts of all words and word pairs (occurring in a sliding window of length 14) from Subset using the sketch and also the exact counts.

4.2 Comparing CM and CU counts and tradeoff between width and depth

To evaluate the amount of over-estimation in CM and CU counts compared to the true counts, we first group all items (words and word pairs) with same true frequency into a single bucket. We then compute the average relative error in each of these buckets. Since low-frequent items are more prone to errors, making this distinction based on frequency lets us understand the regions in which the algorithm is over-estimating. Average Relative error (ARE) is defined as the average of absolute difference between the predicted and the exact value divided by the exact value over all the items in each bucket.

$$\text{ARE} = \frac{1}{N}\sum_{i=1}^{N}\frac{|\text{Exact}_i - \text{Predicted}_i|}{\text{Exact}_i}$$

Where Exact and Predicted denotes values of exact and CM/CU counts respectively; N denotes the number of items with same counts in a bucket.

In Fig. 3(a), we fixed the number of counters to 50 million with four bytes of memory per each counter (thus it only requires 200 MB of main memory). Keeping the total number of counters fixed, we try different values of depth (2, 3, 5 and 7) of the sketch array and in each case the width is set to $\frac{50M}{d}$. The ARE curves in each case are shown in Fig. 3(a). There are three main observations: First it shows that most of the errors occur on low frequency items. For frequent items, in almost all the different runs the ARE is close to zero. Secondly, it shows that ARE is significantly lower (by a factor of two) for the runs which use conservative update (CUx run) compared to the runs that use direct CM sketch (CMx run). The encouraging observation is that, this holds true for almost all different (width,depth) settings. Thirdly, in our experiments, it shows that using depth of 3 gets comparatively less ARE compared to other settings.

To be more certain about this behavior with respect to different settings of width and depth, we tried another setting by increasing the number of counters to 100 million. The curves in 3(b) follow a pattern which is similar to the previous setting. Low frequency items are more prone to error compared to the frequent ones and employing conservative update reduces the ARE by a factor of two. In this setting, depth 3 and 5 do almost the same and get lowest ARE. In both the experiments, setting the depth to three did well and thus in the rest of the paper we fix this parameter to three.

Fig. 4 studies the effect of the number of counters in the sketch (the size of the two-dimensional sketch array) on the ARE. Using more number of counters decreases the ARE in the counts. This is intuitive because, as the length of each row in the sketch increases, the probability of collision decreases and hence the array is more likely to contain true counts. By using 200 million counters, which is comparable to the length of the stream 230 million (Table. 1), we are able to achieve almost zero ARE over all the counts including the rare ones[5]. Note that the actual space required to represent the exact counts is almost two times more than the memory that we use here because there are 230 million word pairs and on an average each word is eight characters long and requires eight bytes (double the size of an integer). The summary of this Figure is that, if we want to preserve the counts of low-frequent items accurately, then we need counters linear in size of stream.

[4]Though a minor point, it allows to process more text.

[5]Even with other datasets we found that using counters linear in the size of the stream leads to ARE close to zero ∀ counts.

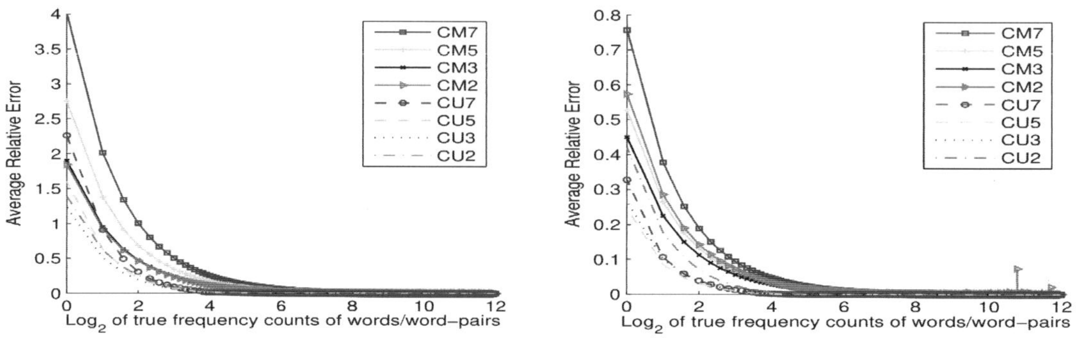

(a) 50M counters

(b) 100M counters

Figure 3: Comparing 50 and 100 million counter models with different (width,depth) settings. The notation CMx represents the Count-Min Sketch with a depth of 'x' and CUx represents the CM sketch along with conservative update and depth 'x'.

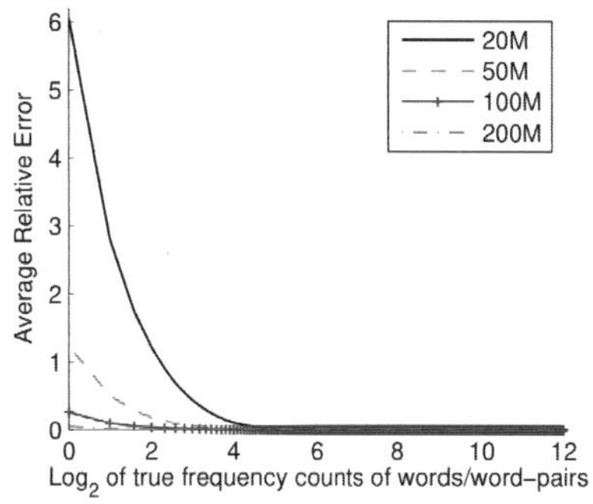

Figure 4: Comparing different size models with depth 3

4.3 Evaluating the CU PMI ranking

In this experiment, we compare the word pairs association rankings obtained using PMI with CU and exact counts. We use two kinds of measures, namely accuracy and Spearman's correlation, to measure the overlap in the rankings obtained by both these approaches.

4.3.1 PointWise Mutual Information

The Pointwise Mutual Information (PMI) (Church and Hanks, 1989) between two words w_1 and w_2 is defined as:

$$PMI(w_1, w_2) = \log_2 \frac{P(w_1, w_2)}{P(w_1)P(w_2)}$$

Here, $P(w_1, w_2)$ is the likelihood that w_1 and w_2 occur together, and $P(w_1)$ and $P(w_2)$ are their independent likelihoods respectively. The ratio between these probabilities measures the degree of statistical dependence between w_1 and w_2.

4.3.2 Description of the metrics

Accuracy is defined as fraction of word pairs that are found in both rankings to the size of top ranked word pairs.

$$\text{Accuracy} = \frac{|\text{CP-WPs} \cap \text{EP-WPs}|}{|\text{EP-WPs}|}$$

Where CP-WPs represent the set of top ranked K word pairs under the counts stored using the CU sketch and EP-WPs represent the set of top ranked word pairs with the exact counts.

Spearman's rank correlation coefficient (ρ) computes the correlation between the ranks of each observation (i.e. word pairs) on two variables (that are top N CU-PMI and exact-PMI values). This measure captures how different the CU-PMI ranking is from the Exact-PMI ranking.

$$\rho = 1 - \frac{6 \sum d_i^2}{F(F^2 - 1)}$$

Where d_i is the difference between the ranks of a word pair in both rankings and F is the number of items found in both sets.

Intuitively, accuracy captures the number of word pairs that are found in both the sets and then Spearman's correlation captures if the relative order of these common items is preserved in both the rankings. In our experimental setup, both these measures are complimentary to each other and measure different aspects. If the rankings match exactly, then we get an accuracy of 100% and a correlation of 1.

4.3.3 Comparing CU PMI ranking

The results with respect to different sized counter (50, 100 and 200 million) models are shown in Table 2. Table 2 shows that having counters linear

Counters	50M		100M		200M	
Top K	*Acc*	ρ	*Acc*	ρ	*Acc*	ρ
50	.20	-0.13	.68	.95	.92	1.00
100	.18	.31	.77	.80	.96	.95
200	.21	.68	.73	.86	.97	.99
500	.24	.31	.71	.97	.95	.99
1000	.33	.17	.74	.87	.95	.98
5000	.49	.38	.82	.82	.96	.97

Table 2: Evaluating the PMI rankings obtained using CM Sketch with conservative update (CU) and Exact counts

in size of stream ($230M$) results in better ranking (i.e. close to the exact ranking). For example, with $200M$ counters, among the top 50 word pairs produced using the CU counts, we found 46 pairs in the set returned by using exact counts. The ρ score on those word pairs is 1 means that the ranking of these 46 items is exactly the same on both CU and exact counts. We see the same phenomena for $200M$ counters with other Top K values. While both accuracy and the ranking are decent with $100M$ counters, if we reduce the number of counters to say $50M$, the performance degrades.

Since, we are not throwing away any infrequent items, PMI will rank pairs with low frequency counts higher (Church and Hanks, 1989). Hence, we are evaluating the PMI values for rare word pairs and we need counters linear in size of stream to get almost perfect ranking. Also, using counters equal to half the length of the stream is decent. However, in some NLP problems, we are not interested in low-frequency items. In such cases, even using space less than linear in number of counters would suffice. In our extrinsic evaluations, we show that using space less than the length of the stream does not degrades the performance.

5 Extrinsic Evaluations

5.1 Experimental Setup

To evaluate the effectiveness of CU-PMI word association scores, we infer semantic orientation (S0) of a word from CU-PMI and Exact-PMI scores. Given a word, the task of finding the SO (Turney and Littman, 2002) of the word is to identify if the word is more likely to be used in positive or negative sense. We use a similar framework as used by the authors[6] to infer the SO. We take the seven positive words (good, nice, excellent, positive, fortunate, correct, and superior) and the negative words (bad, nasty, poor, negative, unfortunate, wrong, and inferior) used in (Turney and Littman, 2002) work. The SO of a given word is calculated based on the strength of its association with the seven positive words, and the strength of its association with the seven negative words. We compute the SO of a word "w" as follows:

$$\begin{aligned}\text{SO-PMI(w)} &= PMI(+,w) - PMI(-,w)\\ \text{PMI(+,w)} &= \sum_{p \in Pwords} \log \frac{\text{hits}(p,w)}{\text{hits}(p) \cdot \text{hits}(w)}\\ \text{PMI(-,w)} &= \sum_{n \in Nwords} \log \frac{\text{hits}(n,w)}{\text{hits}(n) \cdot \text{hits}(w)}\end{aligned}$$

Where, Pwords and Nwords denote the seven positive and negative prototype words respectively.

We compute SO score from different sized corpora (Section 4.1). We use the General Inquirer lexicon[7] (Stone et al., 1966) as a benchmark to evaluate the semantic orientation scores similar to (Turney and Littman, 2002) work. Words with multiple senses have multiple entries in the lexicon, we merge these entries for our experiment. Our test set consists of 1619 positive and 1989 negative words. Accuracy is used as an evaluation metric and is defined as the fraction of number of correctly identified SO words.

$$\text{Accuracy} = \frac{\text{Correctly Identified SO Words} * 100}{\text{Total SO words}}$$

5.2 Results

We evaluate SO of words on three different sized corpora: Gigaword (GW) 6.2GB, GigaWord + 50% of web data (GW+WB1) 21.2GB and GigaWord + 100% of web data (GW+WB2) 31GB. Note that computing the exact counts of all word pairs on these corpora is not possible using main memory, so we consider only those pairs in which one word appears in the prototype list and the other word appears in the test set.

We compute the exact PMI (denoted using Exact) scores for pairs of test-set words w_1 and prototype words w_2 using the above data-sets. To compute PMI, we count the number of hits of individual words w_1 and w_2 and the pair (w_1,w_2) within a sliding window of sizes 10 and 14 over these datasets. After computing the PMI scores, we compute SO score for a word using SO-PMI equation from Section 5.1. If this score is positive, we predict the word as positive. Otherwise, we predict it as

[6]We compute this score slightly differently. However, our main focus is to show that CU-PMI scores are useful.

[7]The General Inquirer lexicon is freely available at http://www.wjh.harvard.edu/ inquirer/

Model		Accuracy window 10			Accuracy window 14		
#of counters	*Mem. Usage*	*GW*	*GW+WB1*	*GW+WB2*	*GW*	*GW+WB1*	*GW+WB2*
Exact	n/a	**64.77**	**75.67**	**77.11**	**64.86**	**74.25**	**75.30**
500M	2GB	62.98	71.09	72.31	63.21	69.21	70.35
1B	4GB	62.95	73.93	75.03	63.95	72.42	72.73
2B	**8GB**	**64.69**	**75.86**	**76.96**	**65.28**	**73.94**	**74.96**

Table 3: Evaluating Semantic Orientation of words with different # of counters of CU sketch with increasing amount of data on window size of 10 and 14. Scores are evaluated using Accuracy metric.

negative. The results on inferring correct SO for a word w with exact PMI (Exact) are summarized in Table 3. It (the second row) shows that increasing the amount of data improves the accuracy of identifying the SO of a word with both the window sizes. The gain is more prominent when we add 50% of web data in addition to Gigaword as we get an increase of more than 10% in accuracy. However, when we add the remaining 50% of web data, we only see an slight increase of 1% in accuracy[8]. Using words within a window of 10 gives better accuracy than window of 14.

Now, we use our CU Sketches of 500 million ($500M$), 1 billion ($1B$) and 2 billion ($2B$) counters to compute CU-PMI. These sketches contain the number of hits of all words/word pairs (not just the pairs of test-set and prototype words) within a window size of 10 and 14 over the whole dataset. The results in Table 3 show that even with CU-PMI scores, the accuracy improves by adding more data. Again we see a significant increase in accuracy by adding 50% of web data to Gigaword over both window sizes. The increase in accuracy by adding the rest of the web data is only 1%.

By using 500M counters, accuracy with CU-PMI are around 4% worse than the Exact. However, increasing the size to $1B$ results in only 2 % worse accuracy compared to the Exact. Going to $2B$ counters (8 GB of RAM), results in accuracy almost identical to the Exact. These results hold almost the same for all the data-sets and for both the window sizes. The increase in accuracy comes at expense of more memory Usage. However, 8GB main memory is not large as most of the conventional desktop machines have this much RAM. The number of $2B$ counters is less than the length of stream for all the data-sets. For GW, GW+WB1 and GW+WB2, $2B$ counters are 10, 20 and 30 times smaller than the stream size. This shows that using counters less than the stream length does not degrade the performance.

[8]These results are similar to the results reported in (Turney and Littman, 2002) work.

The advantage of using Sketch is that it contains counts for all words and word pairs. Suppose we are given a new word to label it as positive or negative. We can find its exact PMI in two ways: First, we can go over the whole corpus and compute counts of this word with positive and negative prototype words. This procedure will return PMI in time needed to traverse the whole corpus. If the corpus is huge, this could be too slow. Second option is to consider storing counts of all word pairs but this is not feasible as their number increases rapidly with increase in data (see Fig. 1). Therefore, using a CM sketch is a very good alternative which returns the PMI in constant time by using only 8GB of memory. Additionally, this Sketch can easily be used for other NLP applications where we need word-association scores.

6 Conclusion

We have explored the idea of the CM Sketch, which approximates the frequency of a word pair in the corpus without explicitly storing the word pairs themselves. We used the idea of a conservative update with the CM Sketch to reduce the average relative error of its approximate counts by a factor of 2. It is an efficient, small-footprint method that scales to at least 37 GB of web data in just 2 billion counters (8 GB main memory). In our extrinsic evaluations, we found that CU Sketch is as effective as exact PMI scores.

Word-association scores from CU Sketch can be used for other NLP tasks like word sense disambiguation, speech and character recognition. The counts stored in CU Sketch can be used to construct small-space randomized language models. In general, this sketch can be used for any application where we want to query a count of an item.

Acknowledgments

We thank the anonymous reviewers for helpful comments. This work is partially funded by NSF grant IIS-0712764 and Google Research Grant Grant for Large-Data NLP.

References

Eneko Agirre, Enrique Alfonseca, Keith Hall, Jana Kravalova, Marius Paşca, and Aitor Soroa. 2009. A study on similarity and relatedness using distributional and wordnet-based approaches. In *NAACL '09: Proceedings of Human Language Technologies: The 2009 Annual Conference of the North American Chapter of the Association for Computational Linguistics*.

Thorsten Brants, Ashok C. Popat, Peng Xu, Franz J. Och, and Jeffrey Dean. 2007. Large language models in machine translation. In *Proceedings of the 2007 Joint Conference on Empirical Methods in Natural Language Processing and Computational Natural Language Learning (EMNLP-CoNLL)*.

Moses Charikar, Kevin Chen, and Martin Farach-colton. 2002. Finding frequent items in data streams.

K. Church and P. Hanks. 1989. Word Association Norms, Mutual Information and Lexicography. In *Proceedings of the 27th Annual Meeting of the Association for Computational Linguistics*, pages 76–83, Vancouver, Canada, June.

Graham Cormode and Marios Hadjieleftheriou. 2008. Finding frequent items in data streams. In *VLDB*.

Graham Cormode and S. Muthukrishnan. 2004. An improved data stream summary: The count-min sketch and its applications. *J. Algorithms*.

Cristian Estan and George Varghese. 2002. New directions in traffic measurement and accounting. *SIGCOMM Comput. Commun. Rev.*, 32(4).

Amit Goyal, Hal Daumé III, and Suresh Venkatasubramanian. 2009. Streaming for large scale NLP: Language modeling. In *North American Chapter of the Association for Computational Linguistics (NAACL)*.

D. Graff. 2003. English Gigaword. Linguistic Data Consortium, Philadelphia, PA, January.

Abby Levenberg and Miles Osborne. 2009. Stream-based randomised language models for SMT. In *Proceedings of the 2009 Conference on Empirical Methods in Natural Language Processing*, pages 756–764, Singapore, August. Association for Computational Linguistics.

Ping Li and Kenneth W. Church. 2007. A sketch algorithm for estimating two-way and multi-way associations. *Comput. Linguist.*, 33(3).

G. S. Manku and R. Motwani. 2002. Approximate frequency counts over data streams. In *Proceedings of the 28th International Conference on Very Large Data Bases*.

S. Muthukrishnan. 2005. Data streams: Algorithms and applications. *Foundations and Trends in Theoretical Computer Science*, 1(2).

Patrick Pantel, Eric Crestan, Arkady Borkovsky, Ana-Maria Popescu, and Vishnu Vyas. 2009. Web-scale distributional similarity and entity set expansion. In *Proceedings of the 2009 Conference on Empirical Methods in Natural Language Processing*, pages 938–947, Singapore, August. Association for Computational Linguistics.

S. Patwardhan and E. Riloff. 2006. Learning Domain-Specific Information Extraction Patterns from the Web. In *Proceedings of the ACL 2006 Workshop on Information Extraction Beyond the Document*.

Deepak Ravichandran, Patrick Pantel, and Eduard Hovy. 2005. Randomized algorithms and nlp: using locality sensitive hash function for high speed noun clustering. In *ACL '05: Proceedings of the 43rd Annual Meeting on Association for Computational Linguistics*.

Florin Rusu and Alin Dobra. 2007. Statistical analysis of sketch estimators. In *SIGMOD '07*. ACM.

Philip J. Stone, Dexter C. Dunphy, Marshall S. Smith, and Daniel M. Ogilvie. 1966. *The General Inquirer: A Computer Approach to Content Analysis*. MIT Press.

David Talbot and Miles Osborne. 2007. Smoothed Bloom filter language models: Tera-scale LMs on the cheap. In *Proceedings of the 2007 Joint Conference on Empirical Methods in Natural Language Processing and Computational Natural Language Learning (EM NLP-CoNLL)*.

Peter D. Turney and Michael L. Littman. 2002. Unsupervised learning of semantic orientation from a hundred-billion-word corpus. *CoRR*, cs.LG/0212012.

Peter D. Turney. 2008. A uniform approach to analogies, synonyms, antonyms, and associations. In *Proceedings of COLING 2008*.

Benjamin Van Durme and Ashwin Lall. 2009a. Probabilistic counting with randomized storage. In *IJCAI'09: Proceedings of the 21st international jont conference on Artifical intelligence*, pages 1574–1579.

Benjamin Van Durme and Ashwin Lall. 2009b. Streaming pointwise mutual information. In *Advances in Neural Information Processing Systems 22*.

Building Webcorpora of Academic Prose with BootCaT

George L. Dillon
University of Washington
PO Box 354330
Seattle, Washington, USA
dillon@u.washington.edu

Abstract

A procedure is described to gather corpora of academic writing from the web using BootCaT. The procedure uses terms distinctive of different registers and disciplines in COCA to locate and gather web pages containing them.

1 Introduction

This is a preliminary report of the results of a new procedure for building a webcorpus of academic writing using BootCaT seeded searches (Baroni and Bernardini, 2004). The procedure inverts the usual one of finding text-internal traits that correlate with externally defined corpora and subcorpora (Lee, 2001). Instead, we seek words and lexical bundles so distinctive of a text-type ("register") that they will induce BootCaT to download texts of that type and no other. In the initial phase, a list of search seed terms is developed to download academic texts; in the second phase, this procedure is refined to increase its resolution, developing search seeds that can bring in texts belonging to sub-types such as Science and Technology, Arts and Humanities, History and Political Science, and so on.

One might object that this is a solution to a non-problem: that all that is necessary is to limit searches to the `.edu` and `.ac.uk` domains to search for academic web texts, at least for US and UK academics. It will become clear, however, that quite a number of qualifying texts can be found elsewhere in other web domains such as `.org`, `.gov`, and even `.com`.

2 Definitions

2.1 Academic writing:

Academic writing is very much a commonsense (or "folk") category. There is considerable agreement that it has research articles and books for disciplinary audiences at its core, but how much more beyond that is in question. This study will draw on three corpus-based studies:

- Coxhead's Academic Word List (AWL; 2000) is drawn from a corpus of 3.5 million words of running text in 441 samples. It is sorted into four equally represented domains (Arts, Commerce, Law, and Science). AWL gives lists of key academic words and word families stratified by frequency in the corpus.
- Biber et al.'s (1999) reference corpus for their lists of academic lexical bundles is a 5.5 million word corpus of articles and sections from books (in equal halves) with a few textbooks for lay readers included. This they further divide into 13 disciplines. Academic is one of four main partitions (which they call 'registers')[1]
- Davies' Corpus of Contemporary American English (COCA) (n.d.). which divides contemporary English into five meta-types, with Academic as one of the five (80 million words)[2]. It

[1]The others are Conversation, Fiction, and News.
[2]The others are Spoken, Fiction, (popular) Magazines, Newspaper and Academic.

Proceedings of the NAACL HLT 2010 Sixth Web as Corpus Workshop, pages 26–31,
Los Angeles, California, June 2010.

is made up entirely of articles in specialist journals and in a few high-brow general interest periodicals (*American Scholar, Raritan Review, Literary Review, Cato Journal).* It includes more disciplines (Religion, Fisheries, Photography, Military Science, Agriculture) and is sorted by Library of Congress top headings (A=General Works, B=Philosophy, Psychology, Religion, etc.) consolidated into eight groupings: Education, History, Geog/SocSci, Law/PolSci, Humanities, Phil/Rel, Sci/Tech, Medicine, Misc (=LC A+Z). These eight parts are searchable, so that we can determine for any expression not just whether it is distinctively academic, but what subtype or types it is distinctive of.

COCA is thus built along principles very similar to those of AWL and Biber et al.'s reference corpus, though it is 2 orders of magnitude larger than either. We would expect AWL words and Biber et al.'s distinctively academic lexical bundles also to be distinctively academic in COCA.

2.2 "Distinctive of"

Here are two lists of words and bundles that we can check for distinctiveness in COCA:

AWL	LGSWE
hypothesis	as we have seen
empirical	extent to which
constrain	has been shown
a priori	has been suggested that
ideology	interesting to note
bias	in the development of
concurrent	no significant difference
intrinsic	presence or absence of
whereas	was found that
qualitative	

Table 1: Academic Key Words (starter set)

Each of these expressions occurs over four times more frequently in the COCA Academic register than any other and twice as frequently there as in all the others combined. Let that be the working definition of "distinctive." So for example, *the presence or absence of* occurs 3.72 times per million words in the COCA Academic subcorpus, 0.35 times per million in the Magazines, and negligibly in Spoken, Fiction, and Newspapers. It is thus 10 times more frequent in the Academic subcorpus than in Magazines and passes the 4 times or more criterion for distinctiveness. In addition, some frequent AWL words were checked for combining in bigrams, which have the potential of being even more specific for domain/genre than individual words. These indeed prove to be more distinctive than the individual words (though of course less frequent). In the first column of Table 2 are the frequencies per million words of these words, phrases, and bigrams in COCA.

words seeds	COCA	words	bundl	bigram	wikiped
hypothesis	74	x	145	140	23
empirical	58	x	30	189	8
constrain	5.5	x	3	10	1
a priori	7	x	3	15	1
ideology	58	x	6	12	16
bias	46	x	41	45	13
concurrent	11	x	10	20	5
intrinsic*	27	x	43	*	6
whereas	105	x	237	114	46
qualitative	38	x	22	109	3
Total (minus intrinsic)	402		498	655	122
acad_bundle					
as we have seen	6	9	x	2	0
extent to which	37	40	x	47	3
has been shown	9	11	x	30	4
has been suggested that	3	4	x	3	6
It is interesting to note	5	5	x	4	3
in the development of	19	16	x	30	10
no significant difference	8	4	x	6	0
presence or absence of	4	4	x	7	1
it was found that	5	2	x	9	2
Total	96	95		137	29
bigrams					
face validity	2	5	1	x	0
these data	18	16	98	x	1
important implications	5	4	5	x	0
basic concepts	2	4	0	x	1
theoretical framework	5	5	1	x	0
intrinsic motivation	6	*	3	x	0
these findings	32	19	75	x	1
this interpretation	6	13	4	x	3
previous work	3	3	11	x	1
indicative of	11	7	15	x	3
Total (minus intrinsic)	89	75	214		10

Table 2: Frequency/Million of Seeds in COCA, Wikipedia,[3] and the Collected Web Corpora

The next three columns give the frequencies/million words of these distinctive terms in each of the three corpora collected from the Web with words, bundles, and bigrams for seeds. (The x's replace the frequencies of the seed terms in the respective

[3]from Corpuseye's 115M word Wikipedia A, B, C corpus at http://corp.hum.sdu.dk/cqp.en.html

corpora made with them—the numbers are of course very high.) These frequencies track those of the terms in the COCA Academic subcorpus quite closely, especially the 'words' corpus, with the 'bundle' and 'bigram' corpora following the same pattern but at somewhat higher (i.e., 'richer') levels.

The Wikipedia figures are included for comparison. The low frequency of these marker words and phrases suggests that Wikipedia is not very academic in its style, which is perhaps not surprising since Wikipedia authors are not allowed to report their own research or argue positions.

Most of these putative marker terms are well represented across the eight academic domains (the “spread” is good). A word that occurs only in one domain will appear to be distinctively academic, but that is a misleading impression. *Stent,* for example, occurs only in the Medical domain in COCA (along with many other terms: *stenosis, mitral*—the list is very long). Even when the match of word and domain is not so clear cut, there are words and phrases that are found preponderantly in a discipline or group of disciplines (a “division” in university parlance) such as *the text itself* and *early modern,* both Art/Humanities terms, and similarly *of the nature of,* which scarcely occurs in Science or Medicine and only infrequently in Geography and Social Science. The next phase of this project will take up the question of increasing the resolution down to the level of a subdomain where a particular set of terms **is** distinctive.

3 Details of Constructing the Web Corpora

These three groups of seed terms were used to make BootCaT tuples (3) and to find URLs of files which contained all three terms of a tuple (with 20 tuples each) and 40 documents for each tuple. Each list of URLs was downloaded and cleaned of CSS style sheets: duplicates and dead-end (e. g., passworded) sites were removed, along with unconverted `.pdf` files. (Yahoo! rather than Google was used because Yahoo! filtered out most of the `.pdfs` and `.doc` files. BootCaT was not too successful converting `.pdf` files: a number of them seemed non-standard or corrupt).
At 3.4 million words, the 'single word' corpus was the largest and had the most pages; the 'bundles' corpus was intermediate in word count but had the fewest pages. The corpus made with the bigram seeds was notably shorter (2.2 million words), but it was very efficient at bringing in occurrences of seed terms from the other sets. The seed terms from all sets were used to cross-check (probe) for occurrence in the other two corpora. These results are given in Table 2 in the second and third columns. There was no overlap of files (i. e., no files in common) in the three downloaded Web corpora and only one overlap between probe term (intrinsic) and file seed (intrinsic motivation).

A further set of lexical bundles (not used as seeds) were run as probes and produced the same pattern (See Table 3). Most of these are *it*-impersonal constructions, and it is not news that academic writing cultivates the impersonal (though it does allow a little *we* plural first person to slip in); in fact, at this proof-of-concept stage, expected findings are confirmation that the collected corpora have the properties of academic writing as we know it across many distinctive lexical bundles, not just the ones used as seeds.

lexical bundles	COCA	20words40	20bun40	bigram4
it should be noted	13	14	16	19
It is possible that	16	22	49	13
it is necessary to	11	16	9	13
it is important to	39	39	30	55
as we shall see	4	1	5	1
it can be seen that	1	1	2	1
in the context of	44	49	28	70
the degree to whicl	19	16	15	27
of the nature of	7	13	7	12
in this paper	14	27	24	53
Total	188	198	182	264

Table 3: Further probes of the 3 Collected Web Corpora
Again, the three web corpora track COCA very closely, with the 'bigram' corpus as the most efficient.

4 Analysis of Web Corpora

4.1 Top-level domains

Table 4 shows that these corpora draw from several web top-level domains, with `.com` either first or second in rank for the three corpora. (The top four domains account for a little over 90% of the pages.)

3 Webcorpora	20word40	20bun40	bigrams4
CURRENT URL	636	464	556
tokens	3.4M	2.8M	2.23M
tokens/url	5346	6034	4011
.org/	182	245	127
.edu/	174	36	163
.com/	197	113	176
.gov/	27	32	46
.net/	35	13	18
.ca/	19	4	15
.de/	19	13	11
.ac.uk/	6	3	7
.ca/	23	5	18

Table 4: Size of Corpora and Range of Domains (Estimated Domain Counts)

The domain counts are estimated, since a `grep` search over-counts by including URLs referred to on the page as well as that of the page itself. These figures are estimated from the URLs in the "cleaned_urls_list" that is used to download the pages. Clearly the `.edu` top-level domain is not the only or even the most productive source of pages containing the search key words. If these are indeed pages of academic writing, then quite a lot of academic writing on the web would get filtered out by using an `.edu` domain filter and a great deal filtered out using `ac.uk`.

4.2 Types of sites

The 1656 downloaded pages came from a wide range of sites. 281 URLs had words such as *article, journal, paper, research, publication,* or other term that identified the contents as scholarly articles. On the other hand, there were 26 entries from `en.wikipedia.org/wiki/`; 17 pages had the word *blog* in their URL and 17 had the word *courses,* the latter being teaching sites with handouts. There were nine pages of customer reviews from `www.amazon.com/review` and 15 pages from `plato.stanford.edu/entries` which is an encyclopedia of philosophy. All of these sites might be said to be academic in a looser sense, the Amazon reviews being the most distant.

5.0 The Next Phase: Increasing Resolution

It is probably only a minority of 'academic' terms that are commonly used across the board in all disciplines (or groups of disciplines). All disciplines use *have argued,* presumably because argument is at the core of academic endeavor and because the present perfect is just right for summarizing other people's claims and your own. And similarly, all disciplines have, or agree they should have, a *theoretical framework.* But one does NOT write *I argue* in Medicine, or so COCA records, nor has the word *interpretive* any use in Medicine, though it is widely used in all the other disciplines. On the other hand, Medicine has its own distinctive bundles including *it is known that*, and *it has been shown/suggested that* (Oakey, 2002)[4].

It is fairly easy to gather terms that appear to be distinctive of a certain discipline, or group of disciplines, to use them to build web corpora like the ones illustrated here, and to take frequent terms from the gathered corpora to do another search within the discipline/domain, and so to build larger and more differentiated corpora that match the COCA/Library of Congress groupings of disciplines much as has been reported here for 'Academic' writing as such. 'Distinctive' can be less stringently defined in this application: a term is distinctive in an academic subdomain when it is distinctively academic and is at least twice as frequent in the subdomain as in the Academic domain as a whole. The terms still have a strong selective effect because when used in triplets, their selective weights are as it were multiplied.

For example, the left column of Table 5 has a set of search seed terms distinctive of texts in the COCA 'Phil/Rel' subcorpus (LC: B).[5] The right column gives a set of search seeds selected from the first 100-300 most frequent words in the corpus made with the initial set of seeds. (Very frequent terms were checked as possible bigram members and the bigram used instead in the actual download of the second corpus.)

[4]Oakey's model study is based on data from the BNC. Some of his discipline-distinctive patterns scarcely occur in the much larger COCA (e. g, *it is found/concluded that*).

[5]It actually includes Philosophy, Religion, and Psychology.

Initial set of seeds	Second, derived set of seeds
this interpretation	phenomenal consciousness
incomprehensible	methodology
dialectic	scientific theories
situational	reductionist
hermeneutics	incoherent
intelligible	in this sense
materialism	in principle
	means that

Table 5: First and Second Seed Sets for Phil/Rel

The two resulting lists of URLs overlapped only slightly. By using each corpus as reference for a keyword search of the other, the terms most distinctive of each (vis-a-vis the other) were extracted. These terms fall into fairly distinct clusters: The first corpus leans toward hermeneutics/interpretation and toward marxism (via *dialectic* and *materialism*)—in short, a course in Continental philosophy (sample key words: *historical consciousness, Marx, Gadamer, bourgeois, class struggle, Scripture, exegesis*). The second has *Dennett* and *falsifiable* as keys and leans toward Anglo-American philosophy of science and of mind (other key words: *qualia, representational contents, mental states, argument for/against, sensory experience, physicalism)*. Here we begin to tap into key terms and themes of various schools of thought within and overlapping disciplines.

It is possible to determine which of the seed tuplets brought in the key phrases; i. e., the strength of particular seeds as attractors of other terms. It can also be determined when a particular web page is causing a term to spike, which happens fairly often in academic writing, since it favors frequent repetition of the key concepts of the article.

These clusters reflect dependencies (or co-locations) within texts rather than within local 'frames' of contiguous words—which is to say registers of the particular disciplines/subdisciplines. Proceeding in this way, specific lists of terms and also turns of phrase for these disciplines can be extracted. This phase of the project is nearing completion.

The power of BootCaT tuplet search to collect corpora rich in the features of academic registers is remarkable, and its potential uses are many.

References

M. Baroni and S. Bernardini. 2004. BootCaT: Bootstrapping corpora and terms from the web. Proceedings of LREC 2004.

D. Biber, S. Johansson, G. Leech, S. Conrad, and E. Finegan. Longman Grammar of Spoken and Written English. Longman, 1999.

A. Coxhead. 2000. A New Academic Word List. TESOL Quarterly, 34(2): 213-238.
_______, n.d. On-line AWL lists. http://www.victoria.ac.nz/lals/resources/academicwordlist/sublists.aspx

M. Davies. n.d. Corpus of Contemporary American English (COCA) www.americancorpus.org.

D. YW. Lee. 2001. Genres, Registers, Text Types, Do mains, and Styles: Clarifying the Concepts and Nav igating a Path Through the BNC Jungle. Language Learning & Technology 5(3): 37-72.

D. Oakey. 2004. Formulaic Language in English Academic Writing. in R. Reppen, S. M. Fitzmaurice, and Douglas Biber, eds. Using Corpora to Explore Linguistic Variation. John Benjamins. 2004.

This page intentionally left blank.

Google Web 1T 5-Grams Made Easy (but not for the computer)

Stefan Evert
Institute of Cognitive Science
University of Osnabrück
49069 Osnabrück, Germany
`stefan.evert@uos.de`

Abstract

This paper introduces *Web1T5-Easy*, a simple indexing solution that allows interactive searches of the Web 1T 5-gram database and a derived database of quasi-collocations. The latter is validated against co-occurrence data from the BNC and ukWaC on the automatic identification of non-compositional VPC.

1 Introduction

The *Google Web 1T 5-gram* (Web1T5) database (Brants and Franz, 2006) consists of frequency counts for bigram, trigrams, 4-grams and 5-grams extracted from 1 trillion words of English Web text, i.e. from a corpus 10,000 times the size of the British National Corpus (Aston and Burnard, 1998). While primarily designed as a resource to build better language models for machine translation and other NLP applications, its public release in 2006 was greeted with great enthusiasm by many researchers in computational linguistics. As one example, Mitchell et al. (2008) used the Web1T5 data successfully to predict fMRI neural activation associated with concrete noun concepts.

For linguistic applications, though, the Web1T5 database presents three major obstacles:

(i) The lack of linguistic annotation: Google's tokenisation splits hyphenated compounds (e.g., *part-time* is split into a three-token sequence *part*|-|*time*) and differs in many other ways from the rules used in liguistic corpora. The n-grams are neither annotated with part-of-speech tags nor lemmatised, and there are separate entries for sentence-initial uppercase and the corresponding lowercase forms.

(ii) The application of frequency thresholds: Despite the enormous size of the database, its compilers found it necessary to omit low-frequency n-grams with fewer than 40 occurrences. This means that non-adjacent word combinations are listed only if the occur in a relatively frequent pattern. As a consequence, it is impossible to obtain reliable frequency estimates for latent phenomena by pooling data (e.g. the co-occurrence frequency of a particular verb with nouns denoting animals).

(iii) The difficulty of interactive search: The complete Web1T5 database consists of 24.4 GiB of binary-sorted, compressed text files. While this format is suitable for building n-gram language models and other offline processing, searching the database is not efficient enough for interactive use. Except for simple, case-sensitive prefix searches – which can be restricted to a single file containing 50–90 MiB of compressed text – every query requires a linear scan of the full database.

This paper presents a simple open-source software solution to the third problem, called *Web1T5-Easy*. The n-gram data are encoded and indexed in a relational database. Building on convenient open-source tools such as SQLite and Perl, the software aims to strike a good balance between search efficiency and ease of use and implementation. With its focus on interactive, but accurate search it complements the approximate indexing and batch processing approaches of Hawker et al. (2007). *Web1T5-Easy* can be downloaded from `http://webascorpus.sf.net/Web1T5-Easy/`.[1]

[1] An online demo of the complete Web1T5 database is available at `http://cogsci.uos.de/~korpora/ws/Web1T5/`.

Proceedings of the NAACL HLT 2010 Sixth Web as Corpus Workshop, pages 32–40,
Los Angeles, California, June 2010.

word 1	*word 2*	*word 3*	*f*
supplement	depend	on	193
supplement	depending	on	174
supplement	depends	entirely	94
supplement	depends	on	338
supplement	derived	from	2668
supplement	des	coups	77
supplement	described	in	200

Table 1: Example of Web1T5 3-gram frequency data (excerpt from file `3gm-0088.gz`).

The rest of this paper is organised as follows. Section 2 describes the general system architecture in more detail. Section 3 explains how collocations (with a maximal span size of four tokens) and distributional semantic models (DSM) can be approximated on the basis of Web1T5 frequency data. Some technical aspects are summarised in Section 4. Section 5 addresses the consequences of problems (i) and (ii). The linguistic usefulness of Web1T5 collocation data is validated on a multiword extraction task from the MWE 2008 workshop.[2] Section 6 concludes with a brief outlook on the future development of Web1T5-Easy.

2 System architecture

While designing the fastest possible indexing architecture for the Web1T5 database is an interesting computer science problem, linguistic applications typically do not require the millisecond response times of a commercial search engine. It is sufficient for interactive queries to be completed within a few seconds, and many users will also be willing to wait several minutes for the result of a complex search operation. Given the tabular format of the Web1T5 n-gram frequency data (cf. Table 1), it was a natural choice to make use of a standard relational database (RDBMS). Database tables can be indexed on single or multiple columns for fast access, and the SQL query languge allows flexible analysis and aggregation of frequency data (see Section 2.2 for some examples). While the indexing procedure can be very time-consuming, it is carried out offline and has to run only once.

[2] `http://multiword.sf.net/mwe2008/`

Web1T5-Easy was designed to balance computational efficiency against implementation effort and ease of use. Its main ingredients are the public-domain embedded relational database engine SQLite and the open-source scripting language Perl which are connected through the portable DBI/DBD interface.[3] The Web1T5-Easy package consists of two sets of Perl scripts. The first set automates pre-processing and indexing, detailed in Section 2.1. The second set, which facilitates command-line access to the database and provides a Web-based GUI, is described in Section 2.2. Technical details of the representation format and performance figures are presented in Section 4.

The embedded database engine SQLite was preferred over a full-fledged RDBMS such as MySQL or PostgreSQL for several reasons: (i) running the database as a user-level process gives better control over huge database files and expensive indexing operations, which might otherwise clog up a dedicated MySQL server computer; (ii) each SQLite database is stored in a single, platform-independent file, so it can easily be copied to other locations or servers; (iii) an embedded database avoids the overhead of exchanging large amounts of data between client and server; (iv) tight integration with the application program allows more flexible use of the database than pure SQL queries (e.g., a Perl script can define its own SQL functions, cf. Section 3).

It is quite possible that the sophisticated query optimisers of MySQL and commercial RDMBS implementations would improve performance on complex SQL queries. Since Web1T5-Easy uses the generic DBI interface, it can easily be adapted to any RDMBS back-end for which DBI/DBD drivers are available.

2.1 The indexing procedure

Indexing of the Web1T5 n-gram data is carried out in four stages:

1. In an optional pre-processing step, words are filtered and normalised to lowercase.[4] Each

[3] See the Web pages at `http://www.sqlite.org/`, `http://www.perl.org/` and `http://dbi.perl.org/`.

[4] The default filter replaces numbers by the code `NUM`, various punctuation symbols by the code `PUN`, and all "messy" strings by the code `UNK`. It can easily be replaced by a user-defined normalisation mapping.

word in an n-gram entry is then coded as a numeric ID, which reduces database size and improves both indexing and query performance (see Section 4 for details on the representation format). The resulting tuples of $n+1$ integers (n word IDs plus frequency count) are inserted into a database table.

2. If normalisation was applied, the table will contain multiple entries for many n-grams.[5] In Stage 2, their frequency counts are aggregated with a suitable SQL query. This is one of the most expensive and disk-intensive operations of the entire indexing procedure.

3. A separate SQL index is created for each n-gram position (e.g., *word 1*, *word 2* and *word 3* in Table 1). Multi-column indexes are currently omitted, as they would drastically increase the size of the database files.[6] Moreover, the use of an index only improves query execution speed if it is highly selective, as explained in Section 4. If desired, the Perl scripts can trivially be extended to create additional indexes.

4. A statistical analysis of the database is performed to improve query optimisation (i.e., appropriate selection of indexes).

The indexing procedure is carried out separately for bigrams, trigrams, 4-grams and 5-grams, using a shared lexicon table to look up numeric IDs. Users who do not need the larger n-grams can easily skip them, resulting in a considerably smaller database and much faster indexing.

2.2 Database queries and the Web GUI

After the SQLite database has been populated and indexed, it can be searched with standard SQL queries (typically a join between one of the n-gram tables and the lexicon table), e.g. using the `sqlite3` command-line utility. Since this requires detailed knowledge of SQL syntax as well as the database layout and normalisation rules, the Web1T5-Easy package offers a simpler, user-friendly query language, which is internally translated into appropriate SQL code.

A Web1T5-Easy query consists of 2–5 search terms separated by blanks. Each search term is either a literal word (e.g. `sit`), a set of words in square brackets (e.g. `[sit,sits,sat,sitting]`), a prefix (`under%`) or suffix (`%ation`) expression, `*` for an arbitrary word, or `?` to skip a word. The difference between the latter two is that positions marked by `*` are included in the query result, while those marked by `?` are not. If a query term cannot match because of normalisation, an informative error message is shown. Matches can be ranked by frequency or by association scores, according to one of the measures recommended by Evert (2008): t-score (t), log-likelihood (G^2), chi-squared with Yates' correction (X^2), pointwise MI, or a version of the Dice coefficient.

For example, the query `web as corpus` shows that the trigram *Web as Corpus* occurs 1,104 times in the Google corpus (case-insensitive). `%ly good fun` lists ways of having fun such as *really good fun* (12,223×), *jolly good fun* (3,730×) and *extremely good fun* (2,788×). The query `[sit,sits,sat,sitting] * ? chair` returns the patterns *SIT in ... chair* (201,084×), *SIT on ... chair* (61,901×), *SIT at ... chair* (1,173×), etc. Corpus frequencies are automatically summed over all fillers in the third slot.

The query implementation is available as a command-line version and as a CGI script that provides a Web-based GUI to the Web1T5-Easy database. The CGI version also offers CSV and XML output formats for use as a Web service.

3 Quasi-collocations and DSM

Many corpus linguists and lexicographers will particularly be interested in using the Web1T5 database as a source of collocations (in the sense of Sinclair (1991)). While the British National Corpus at best provides sufficient data for a collocational analysis of some 50,000 words (taking $f \geq 50$ to be the minimum corpus frequency necessary), Web1T5 offers comprehensive collocation data for almost 500,000

[5] For example, with the default normalisation, *bought 2 bottles*, *bought 5 bottles*, *Bought 3 bottles*, *BOUGHT 2 BOTTLES* and many other trigrams are mapped to the representation *bought NUM bottles*. The database table thus contains multiple entries of the trigram *bought NUM bottles*, whose frequency counts have to be added up.

[6] For the 5-gram table, 10 different two-column indexes would be required to cover a wide range of queries, more than doubling the size of the database file.

Collocates of "corpus" (f=5137372)

50 matches in 0.20 seconds

collocate	t-score	frequency	expected	span distribution (left, right)
christi	1582.37	2504283	198.3	00% 01% 01% ‖ 97% 01% 00%
tx	794.93	639346	3725.8	00% 14% 02% ‖ 00% 16% 67%
habeas	720.32	518962	52.8	00% 00% 99% ‖ 00% 00% 00%
texas	629.04	411495	7978.1	06% 09% 02% ‖ 00% 22% 61%
columbus	429.55	186575	1034.0	48% 16% 36% ‖ 00% 00% 00%
dallas	390.37	156254	1943.7	00% 00% 00% ‖ 00% 70% 30%
writ	372.46	138960	116.1	98% 00% 00% ‖ 01% 00% 00%
callosum	368.99	136174	8.8	01% 00% 00% ‖ 98% 01% 00%
m	327.51	146346	21058.1	45% 46% 08% ‖ 00% 00% 00%
hotels	287.67	114198	16985.0	11% 15% 16% ‖ 00% 52% 05%
luteum	275.98	76176	5.7	02% 00% 00% ‖ 97% 01% 00%
oh	265.20	80036	5009.5	03% 04% 93% ‖ 00% 00% 00%

Figure 1: Quasi-collocations for the node word *corpus* in the Web GUI of Web1T5-Easy.

words (which have at least 50 different collocates in the database, and $f \geq 10{,}000$ in the original Google corpus).

Unfortunately, the Web1T5 distribution does not include co-occurrence frequencies of word pairs, except for data on immediately adjacent bigrams. It is possible, though, to derive approximate co-occurrence frequencies within a collocational span of up to 4 tokens. In this approach, each n-gram table yields information about a specific collocate position relative to the node. For instance, one can use the 4-gram table to identify collocates of the node word *corpus* at position +3 (i.e., 3 tokens to the right of the node) with the Web1T5-Easy query `corpus ? ? *`, and collocates at position −3 (i.e., 3 tokens to the left of the node) with the query `* ? ? corpus`. Co-occurrence frequencies within a collocational span, e.g. $(-3,+3)$, are obtained by summation over all collocate positions in this window, collecting data from multiple n-gram tables.

It has to be kept in mind that such *quasi-collocations* do not represent the true co-occurrence frequencies, since an instance of co-occurrence of two words is counted only if it forms part of an n-gram with $f \geq 40$ that has been included in Web1T5. Especially for larger distances of 3 or 4 tokens, this limitation is likely to discard most of the evidence for co-occurrence and put a focus on collocations that form part of a rigid multiword unit or institutionalised phrase. Thus, *cars* becomes the most salient collocate of *collectibles* merely because the two words appear in the slogan *from collectibles to cars* (9,443,572×). Section 5 validates the linguistic usefulness of Web1T5 quasi-collocations in a multiword extraction task.

Web1T5-Easy compiles frequency data for quasi-collocations in an additional step after the complete n-gram data have been indexed. For each pair of co-occurring words, the number of co-occurrences in each collocational position $(-4,-3,\ldots,+3,+4)$ is recorded. If the user has chosen to skip the largest n-gram tables, only a shorter collocational span will be available.

The Web GUI generates SQL code to determine co-occurrence frequencies within a user-defined collocational span on the fly, by summation over the appropriate columns of the quasi-collocations table. Collocates can be ranked by a range of association measures (t, G^2, X^2, MI, Dice, or frequency f), which are implemented as user-defined SQL functions in the Perl code. In this way, sophisticated statistical analyses can be performed even if they are not directly supported by the RDBMS back-end. Figure 1 shows an example of quasi-collocations in the Web GUI, ranked according to the t-score measure. On the right-hand side of the table, the distribution across collocate positions is visualised.

In computational linguistics, collocations play an important role as the term-term co-occurrence matrix underlying distributional semantic models

size (GiB)	*database file*	*no. of rows*
0.23	`vocabulary`	5,787,556
7.24	`2-grams`	153,634,491
32.81	`3-grams`	594,453,302
64.32	`4-grams`	933,385,623
75.09	`5-grams`	909,734,581
31.73	`collocations`	494,138,116
211.42	*total*	3,091,133,669

Table 2: Size of the fully indexed Web1T5 database, including quasi-collocations.

(DSM), with association scores used as feature weights (see e.g. Curran (2004, Sec. 4.3)). The Web1T5-Easy quasi-collocations table provides a sparse representation of such a term-term matrix, where only 494×10^6 or 0.0015% of the $5.8 \times 10^6 \cdot 5.8 \times 10^6 = 33.5 \times 10^{12}$ cells of a full co-occurrence matrix are populated with nonzero entries.

4 Technical aspects

An essential feature of Web1T5-Easy is the numeric coding of words in the n-gram tables, which allows for compact storage and more efficient indexing of the data than a full character string representation. A separate lexicon table lists every (normalised) word form together with its corpus frequency and an integer ID. The lexicon is sorted by decreasing frequency: since SQLite encodes integers in a variable-length format, it is advantageous to assign low ID numbers to the most frequent terms.

Every table is stored in its own SQLite database file, e.g. `vocabulary` for the lexicon table and `collocations` for quasi-collocations (cf. Section 3). The database files for different n-gram sizes (`2-grams`, `3-grams`, `4-grams`, `5-grams`) share the same layout and differ only in the number of columns. Table 2 lists the disk size and number of rows of each database file, with default normalisation applied. While the total size of 211 GiB by far exceeds the original Web1T5 distribution, it can easily be handled by modern commodity hardware and is efficient enough for interactive queries.

Performance measurements were made on a midrange 64-bit Linux server with 2.6 GHz AMD Opteron CPUs (4 cores) and 16 GiB RAM. SQLite database files and temporary data were stored on a fast, locally mounted hard disk. Similar or better hardware will be available at most academic institutions, and even in recent personal desktop PCs.

Indexing the n-gram tables in SQLite took about two weeks. Since the server was also used for multiple other memory- and disk-intensive tasks during this period, the timings reported here should only be understood as rough indications. The indexing process might be considerably faster on a dedicated server. Roughly equal amounts of time were spent on each of the four stages listed in Section 2.1.

Database analysis in Stage 4 turned out to be of limited value because the SQLite query optimiser was not able to make good use of this information. Therefore, a heuristic optimiser based on individual term frequencies was added to the Perl query scripts. This optimiser chooses the n-gram slot that is most likely to speed up the query, and explicitly disables the use of indexes for all other slots. Unless another constraint is much more selective, preference is always given to the first slot, which represents a clustered index (i.e. database rows are stored in index order) and can be scanned very efficiently.

With these explicit optimisations, Stage 4 of the indexing process can be omitted. If normalisation is not required, Stage 2 can also be skipped, reducing the total indexing time by half.

At first sight, it seems to be easy to compile the database of quasi-collocations one node at a time, based on the fully indexed n-gram tables. However, the overhead of random disk access during index lookups made this approach intractable.[7] A brute-force Perl script that performs multiple linear scans of the complete n-gram tables, holding as much data in RAM as possible, completed the compilation of co-occurrence frequencies in about three days.

Table 3 shows execution times for a selection of Web1T5-Easy queries entered in the Web GUI. In general, prefix queries that start with a reasonably specific term (such as `time of *`) are very fast, even on a cold cache. The query `%ly good fun` is a pathological case: none of the terms is selective enough to make good use of the corresponding

[7] In particular, queries like `* ? ? corpus` that scan for collocates to the left of the node word are extremely inefficient, since the index on the last n-gram slot is not clustered and accesses matching database rows in random order.

Web1T5-Easy query	*cold cache*	*warm cache*
`corpus linguistics`	0.11s	0.01s
`web as corpus`	1.29s	0.44s
`time of *`	2.71s	1.09s
`%ly good fun`	181.03s	24.37s
`[sit,sits,sat,sitting] * ? chair`	1.16s	0.31s
`* linguistics` *(association ranking)*	11.42s	0.05s
`university of *` *(association ranking)*	1.48s	0.48s
collocations of `linguistics`	0.21s	0.13s
collocations of `web`	6.19s	3.89s

Table 3: Performance of interactive queries in the Web GUI of Web1T5-Easy. Separate timings are given for a cold disk cache (first query) and warm disk cache (repeated query). Re-running a query with modified display or ranking settings will only take the time listed in the last column.

index, and entries matching the wildcard expression `%ly` in the first slot are scattered across the entire trigram table.

5 Validation on a MWE extraction task

In order to validate the linguistic usefulness of Web1T5 quasi-collocations, they were evaluated on the English VPC shared task from the MWE 2008 workshop.[8] This data set consists of 3,078 verb-particle constructions (VPC), which have been manually annotated as compositional or non-compositional (Baldwin, 2008). The task is to identify non-compositional VPC as true positives (TP) and re-rank the data set accordingly. Evaluation is carried out in terms of precision-recall graphs, using average precision (AP, corresponding to the area under a precision-recall curve) as a global measure of accuracy.

Frequency data from the Web1T5 quasi-collocations table was used to calculate association scores and rankings. Since previous studies suggest that no single association measure works equally well for all tasks and data sets, several popular measures were included in the evaluation: t-score (t), chi-squared with Yates' continuity correction (X^2), Dice coefficient (Dice), co-occurrence frequency (f), log-likelihood (G^2) and Mutual Information (MI); see e.g. Evert (2008) for full equations and references. The results are compared against rankings obtained from more traditional, linguistically annotated corpora of British English: the balanced, 100-million-word British National Corpus (Aston and Burnard, 1998) and the 2-billion-word Web corpus ukWaC (Baroni et al., 2009).

For BNC and ukWaC, three different extraction methods were used: (i) adjacent *bigrams* of verb + particle/preposition; (ii) shallow *syntactic patterns* based on POS tags (allowing pronouns and simple noun phrases between verb and particle); and (iii) surface co-occurrence within a *collocational span* of 3 tokens to the right of the node $(+1, +3)$, filtered by POS tag. Association scores were calculated using the same measures as for the Web1T5 quasi-collocations. Preliminary experiments with different collocational spans showed consistently lower accuracy than for $(+1, +3)$. In each case, the same association measures were applied as for Web1T5.

Evaluation results are shown in Figure 3 (graphs) and Table 4 (AP). The latter also describes the coverage of the corpus data by listing the number of candidates for which no frequency information is available (second column). These candidates are always ranked at the end of the list. While the BNC has a coverage of 92%–94% (depending on extraction method), scaling up to Web1T5 completely eliminates the missing data problem.

However, identification of non-compositional VPC with the Web1T5 quasi-collocations is considerably less accurate than with linguistically annotated data from the much smaller BNC. For recall values above 50%, the precision of statistical association measures such as t and X^2 is particularly poor

[8] `http://multiword.sf.net/mwe2008/`

	coverage (missing)	average precision (%) t	X^2	*Dice*	f	G^2	*MI*
BNC (bigrams)	242	**30.04**	29.75	27.12	26.55	29.86	22.79
BNC (syntactic patterns)	201	30.42	30.49	27.48	25.87	**30.64**	22.48
BNC (span $+1 \ldots +3$)	185	29.15	**32.12**	30.13	24.33	31.06	22.58
ukWaC (bigrams)	171	29.28	**30.32**	27.79	25.37	29.63	25.13
ukWaC (syntactic patterns)	162	29.20	**31.19**	27.90	24.19	30.06	25.08
ukWaC (span $+1 \ldots +3$)	157	27.82	**32.66**	30.54	23.03	30.01	25.76
Web1T5 (span $+1 \ldots +3$)	3	**25.83**	25.27	25.33	20.88	25.77	20.81
BNC untagged ($+1 \ldots +3$)	39	27.22	27.85	**28.98**	22.51	28.13	19.60

Table 4: Evaluation results for English non-compositional VPC (Baldwin, 2008): average precision (AP) as a global indicator. The baseline AP for random candidate ranking is 14.29%. The best result in each row is highlighted in bold.

(Figure 3.h). On the annotated corpora, where nodes and collocates are filtered by POS tags, best results are obtained with the least constrained extraction method and the chi-squared (X^2) measure. Scaling up to the 2-billion-word ukWaC corpus gives slightly better coverage and precision than on the BNC. Moreover, X^2 is now almost uniformly better than (or equal to) any other measure (Figure 3.f).

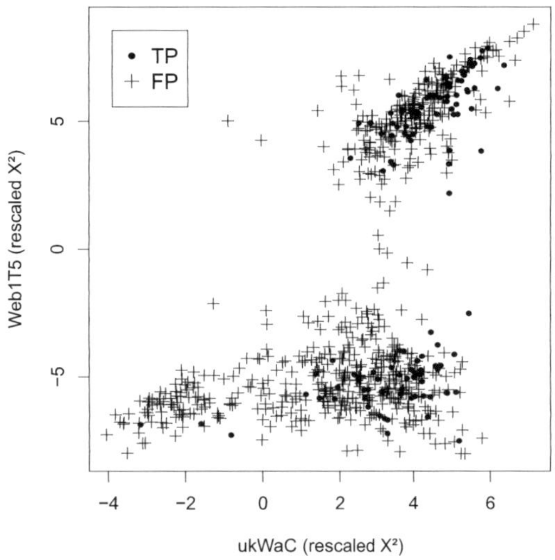

Figure 2: Comparison of X^2 association scores on ukWaC and Web1T5. Axes are rescaled logarithmically, preserving sign to indicate positive vs. negative association.

In order to determine whether the poor performance of Web1T5 is simply due to the lack of linguistic annotation or whether it points to an intrinsic problem of the n-gram database, co-occurrence data were extracted from an untagged version of the BNC using the same method as for the Web1T5 data. While there is a significant decrease in precision (cf. Figure 3.g and the last row of Table 4), the results are still considerably better than on Web1T5. In the MWE 2008 competition, Ramisch et al. (2008) were also unable to improve on the BNC results using a phrase entropy measure based on search engine data.

The direct comparison of X^2 association scores on ukWaC and Web1T5 in Figure 2 reveals that the latter are divided into strongly positive and strongly negative association, while scores on ukWaC are spread evenly across the entire range. It is remarkable that many true positives (TP) exhibit negative association in Web1T5, while all but a few show the expected positive association in ukWaC. This unusual pattern, which may well explain the poor VPC evaluation results, can also be observed for adjacent bigrams extracted from the 2-grams table (not shown). It suggests a general problem of the Web1T5 data that is compounded by the quasi-collocations approach.

6 Future work

A new release of Web1T5-Easy is currently in preparation. It will refactor the Perl code into reusable and customisable modules that can easily be embedded in user scripts and adapted to other databases such as Brants and Franz (2009). We are looking forward to Web1T5 v2, which promises easier indexing and much richer interactive queries.

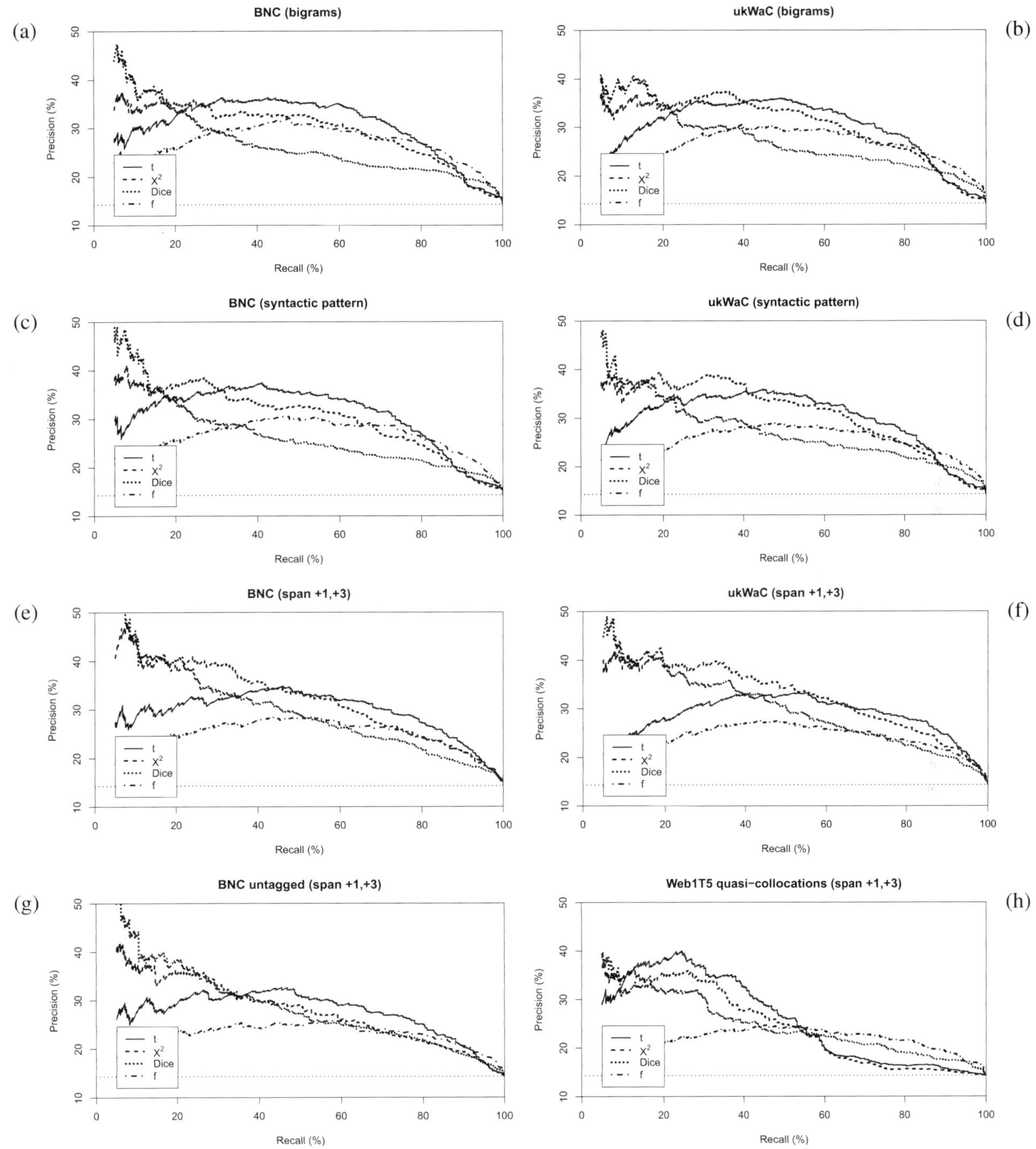

Figure 3: Evaluation results for English non-compositional VPC (Baldwin, 2008): precision-recall graphs. Rankings according to the Web1T5 quasi-collocations are shown in the bottom right panel (h). The baseline precision is 14.29%.

References

Guy Aston and Lou Burnard. 1998. *The BNC Handbook*. Edinburgh University Press, Edinburgh. See also the BNC homepage at http://www.natcorp.ox.ac.uk/.

Timothy Baldwin. 2008. A resource for evaluating the deep lexical acquisition of English verb-particle constructions. In *Proceedings of the LREC Workshop Towards a Shared Task for Multiword Expressions (MWE 2008)*, pages 1–2, Marrakech, Morocco.

Marco Baroni, Silvia Bernardini, Adriano Ferraresi, and Eros Zanchetta. 2009. The WaCky Wide Web: A collection of very large linguistically processed Web-crawled corpora. *Language Resources and Evaluation*, 43(3):209–226.

Thorsten Brants and Alex Franz. 2006. *Web 1T 5-gram Version 1*. Linguistic Data Consortium, Philadelphia, PA. http://www.ldc.upenn.edu/Catalog/CatalogEntry.jsp?catalogId=LDC2006T13.

Thorsten Brants and Alex Franz. 2009. *Web 1T 5-gram, 10 European Languages Version 1*. Linguistic Data Consortium, Philadelphia, PA. http://www.ldc.upenn.edu/Catalog/CatalogEntry.jsp?catalogId=LDC2009T25.

James Richard Curran. 2004. *From Distributional to Semantic Similarity*. Ph.D. thesis, University of Edinburgh.

Stefan Evert. 2008. Corpora and collocations. In Anke Lüdeling and Merja Kytö, editors, *Corpus Linguistics. An International Handbook*, chapter 58. Mouton de Gruyter, Berlin.

Tobias Hawker, Mary Gardiner, and Andrew Bennetts. 2007. Practical queries of a massive n-gram database. In *Proceedings of the Australasian Language Technology Workshop 2007*, pages 40–48, Melbourne, Australia.

Tom M. Mitchell, Svetlana V. Shinkareva, Andrew Carlson, Kai-Min Chang, Vicente L. Malave, Robert A. Mason, and Marcel Adam Just. 2008. Predicting human brain activity associated with the meanings of nouns. *Science*, 320:1191–1195.

Carlos Ramisch, Paulo Schreiner, Marco Idiart, and Aline Villavicencio. 2008. An evaluation of methods for the extraction of multiword expressions. In *Proceedings of the LREC Workshop Towards a Shared Task for Multiword Expressions (MWE 2008)*, pages 50–53, Marrakech, Morocco.

John Sinclair. 1991. *Corpus, Concordance, Collocation*. Oxford University Press, Oxford.

Author Index

Association for Computational Linguistics
209 N. Eighth Street
Stroudsburg, Pennsylvania 18360

CURRAN ASSOCIATES INC
proceedings.com